# HOUSING FOR PEOPLE WITH SIGHT LOSS
## A Thomas Pocklington Trust Design Guide

**Chris Goodman**
Habinteg Housing Association

Under commission from Thomas Pocklington Trust

  Thomas Pocklington Trust
**Housing and support for people with sight loss**

Endorsed by

The Society of Light and Lighting

College of Occupational Therapists

HOUSING CORPORATION

 bre press

Thomas Pocklington Trust, Habinteg Housing Association and the publisher make every effort to ensure the accuracy and quality of information and guidance when it is first published. However, we can take no responsibility for the subsequent use of this information, nor for any errors or omissions that it may contain.

IHS BRE Press supplies a wide range of building and construction-related information products from BRE and other respected organisations. Details are available from:

www.ihsbrepress.com
or
IHS BRE Press
Willoughby Road
Bracknell RG12 8FB
Tel: 01344 328038
Fax: 01344 328005
Email: brepress@ihs.com

Published by IHS BRE Press for
Thomas Pocklington Trust

Requests to copy any part of this publication should be made to the publisher:
IHS BRE Press
Garston, Watford WD25 9XX
Tel: 01923 664761
Email: brepress@ihs.com

**Author's details**
This Guide, commissioned by Thomas Pocklington Trust, has been written by Chris Goodman of Habinteg Housing Association.

Thomas Pocklington Trust
5 Castle Row
Horticultural Place
Chiswick
London W4 4JQ
www.pocklington-trust.org.uk

Chris Goodman
Design & Development Manager
Habinteg Housing Association
Holyer House
20–21 Red Lion Court
London EC4A 3EB
www.habinteg.org.uk

**EP 84**
**© Copyright Thomas Pocklington Trust 2008**
**First published 2008**
**ISBN 978-1-84806-029-6**

# FOREWORD

I very much welcome the publication of this important new guide which forms part of a wider determination to ensure that people with disabilities have the housing opportunities that are designed with their needs and abilities in mind.

It is estimated that some 2 million people in the UK are affected by sight loss in their everyday life. As our society ages, the prevalence of sight loss will inevitably increase. We must make sure that the houses we build in the future all enable people with sight loss to live safely and comfortably at home for as long as possible.

As a government we are committed to 'inclusive design' that meets the needs of all - and that principle should be reflected in all forms of housing investment - whether affordable homes or market sector housing. This is evident not only in Part M of the Building Regulations, but also the adoption of 'Lifetime Homes' standards within many strategic planning strategies.

This technical guide is part of that process to ensure that housing promotes greater opportunity for all. It is based on the latest research. For everyone involved in designing and providing homes, it offers new insight and practical suggestions on how to maximise the functional vision for people affected by sight loss. As such, I am sure it will be welcomed not only by the industry, but in particular, by the people who will live in the homes that are built.

*Kay Andrews*

*Baroness Kay Andrews*
***Parliamentary Under Secretary of State,
Communities and Local Government***

March 2008

# PREFACE

This *Guide* follows research projects commissioned by Thomas Pocklington Trust as part of its continuing research and development programme relating to the needs, experiences, expectations and choices for people with sight loss within their home environment.

The broad outline for the *Guide's* content has been informed extensively from projects commissioned by Thomas Pocklington Trust and undertaken by University College London, principally:

- the housing and support needs of people of working age with sight loss, and
- the housing, care and support needs of older people with sight loss.

Specific guidance on lighting, one of the most crucial issues for people with sight loss, has been drawn from Thomas Pocklington Trust's commissioned studies and trials on the subject, undertaken by the Research Group for Inclusive Environments, The University of Reading.

Thomas Pocklington Trust approached Habinteg Housing Association, as recognised experts in producing practical guidance on inclusive design and disability for architects and developers, to draft a practical *design guide* building on the research reports and using Habinteg's experience as a direct developer of inclusive housing environments.

*Ron Bramley*
**Chief Executive**
**Thomas Pocklington Trust**

*Mike Donnelly*
**Chief Executive**
**Habinteg Housing Association**

March 2008

# ABOUT THOMAS POCKLINGTON TRUST

Thomas Pocklington Trust is the leading provider of housing, care and support services for people with sight loss in the UK. Each year Pocklington also commits around £700 000 to fund social and public health research and development projects.

Pocklington's operations offer a range of sheltered and supported housing, residential care, respite care, day services, home care services, resource centres and community-based support services. Pocklington is working in partnership with local authorities, registered social landlords and other voluntary organisations to expand its range of services.

Pocklington's research and development programme aims to identify practical ways to improve the lives of people with sight loss, by:
- improving social inclusion, independence and quality of life,
- improving and developing service outcomes, as well as
- focusing on public health issues.

# ABOUT HABINTEG HOUSING ASSOCIATION

As well as being a housing provider, Habinteg Housing Association is recognised as the UK's leading authority for housing and disability issues. Since being established in 1970, the Association has always had dual aims:
- the provision of high-quality thoughtfully designed housing and services, and
- the mainstreaming of accessible and inclusive homes and neighbourhoods.

Habinteg helped to develop the Lifetime Homes standard and has also co-authored the *Wheelchair housing design guide*[32].

Habinteg applies its expertise to challenge negative social attitudes, promote the rights of disabled people and improve inclusive design standards within housing.

# ACKNOWLEDGEMENTS

Thomas Pocklington Trust is grateful for the funding given to this project by The Wilberforce Trust.

A Steering Group consisting of the following key individuals gave valuable advice and feedback on the Guide's content based on detailed research findings.

**Professor Julienne Hanson**
*Professor of House Form and Culture, The Bartlett School of Graduate Studies, University College London*
Research carried out by Professor Hanson and her colleagues, sponsored by the Housing Corporation and Thomas Pocklington Trust, has informed the Guide in relation to the general housing and support needs of adults with sight loss.

**Dr Geoff Cook**
*Director of the Research Group for Inclusive Environments, The University of Reading*
Geoff Cook has given specialist advice in relation to lighting issues within the Guide. The University's research, funded by Thomas Pocklington Trust, recorded field studies on lighting conditions and user experiences within a range of homes of blind and partially sighted people.

**Dr Angela McCullagh**
*Research and Development Director, Thomas Pocklington Trust*
Angela McCullagh has had overall responsibility for commissioning the research informing this *Guide*.

**Anthony Slater**
*Lighting Development Manager, Thomas Pocklington Trust*
Formerly Director, Environmental Engineering, BRE, Anthony Slater has provided additional specialist lighting expertise and project management.

**Helen George**
Formerly *Research Manager, Habinteg Housing Association*
Helen George was the initial project manager.

A symposium was also held with practitioners and service users to gain further advice and share experiences. The views of a number of residents regarding their current accommodation were also obtained by direct interview. A list of symposium attendees and interviewees is given below.

*Chairmen:*
Ron Bramley
**Chief Executive**
**Thomas Pocklington Trust**

Mike Donnelly
**Chief Executive**
**Habinteg Housing Association**

*Attendees and interviewees:*
Peter Jenkins
**Ability Housing Association**

Sarah Davis
**Chartered Institute of Housing**

Denis Taylor
**Devon Community Housing Society**

Natalie Salmon
**Disability Rights Commission**

Rebecca Thompson
**Easy Living**

Peter Nicholson
Edwin Trotter
**Edwin Trotter Architects**

Adrian Harden
**Focus Futures**

Alex Perry
Andy Smith (Resident)
Margaret Smith (Resident)
Andrew Young
**Habinteg Housing Association**

Chris McGinley
**Helen Hamlyn Research Centre**

Una Whelan
**In Touch Support/Hyde Housing Association**

David Pearce
**Middlesex Association for the Blind**

Jaqui Wan
**National Housing Federation**

John Wood
**Northamptonshire Association for the Blind**

Maurice Heather
Anne-Marie Nicholson
**PRP Architects**

Dr John Gill
**RNIB**

Stuart Davies
Janet John
**RNIB Cymru**

Paul Garwood
Stephen Kill
Sue Parish
Heather Salisbury
**Seeability**

Michael Reinhold
**St Dunstan's**

Tony James
**Stephen George and Partners**

Dr Pam Thomas
**SURFACE, University of Salford**

Ian Ferguson
**The Beacon Centre for the Blind**

Lawrence Chee
**The Housing Corporation**

Keith McKee
**The Wilberforce Trust**

Kirpal Bilkhu
Sarah Buchanan
Steve Craven
Jill Davies (Resident)
Anne Green
Jan Gresham
David Hall (Resident)
Iain Hopkin
Ennis Killip (Resident)
Lesley Peter (Resident)
Tony Scott (Resident)
Gail Sullivan
Heather Taylor (Resident)
**Thomas Pocklington Trust**

# CONTENTS

## TECHNICAL GUIDANCE

# APPENDICES

# CHAPTER 1
# INTRODUCTION

This *Guide* contains good practice guidance, primarily to assist architects/designers and housing practitioners, in the development of inclusive domestic environments that meet the requirements of people with sight loss. The emphasis is on maximising functional vision and on minimising barriers and risk by achieving specific design and specification requirements. The *Guide* also seeks to promote good design in all housing: a key consideration given the link between the ageing of the population and sight loss.

## 1.1 EYE CONDITIONS

The most common eye conditions and a brief outline of their general effects are described below.

### 1.1.1 Macular degeneration (MD)

This condition is common among older people. There are two types:

- dry MD which develops slowly and currently has no treatment, and

- wet MD in which the extent of vision loss varies enormously but can be very severe.

MD causes progressive loss of central vision. Straight lines can become distorted and blank or dark spots can occur in the centre of the vision.

Difficulty is often experienced in reading, writing, watching television, cooking, sewing, other detailed tasks involving seeing small objects, and recognising faces.

### 1.1.2 Cataract

This condition is a clouding of the lens inside the eye. More than 50% of people over 65 years of age have some degree of cataract.

All aspects of daily living including general mobility, household tasks, recognising faces and night travel can be affected by the blurred or cloudy vision and the increase in dazzle and glare caused by the condition.

Most cataracts can be treated surgically with a good success rate.

### 1.1.3 Glaucoma

Glaucoma describes a group of conditions that cause gradual degeneration of the cells of the optic nerve, which carry information from the eye to the brain.

Glaucoma causes blank patches just off the centre of the visual field. In advanced stages, the field of vision will be narrowed leaving only a small part of the central vision due to the blank patches enlarging and merging, thus giving a tunnel vision effect.

The condition has a major impact on mobility.

### 1.1.4 Retinitis pigmentosa

Retinitis pigmentosa describes a group of hereditary eye disorders.

Sight loss will be gradual but progressive. Functional vision in poor light and the visual field will be reduced.

Detailed tasks and reading become difficult and bright lights and glare are increasingly problematic.

### 1.1.5 Diabetic retinopathy

Diabetic retinopathy is linked to diabetes mellitus (Type 1 diabetes) and affects the fine network of blood vessels in the retina. There are two types:

- *Maculopathy* affects the central vision. Recognising faces, seeing fine detail and reading small print is difficult.

- *Proliferative retinopathy* is rarer and causes blurred and patchy eyesight. Without treatment, it can cause total loss of vision.

All these eye conditions will affect individuals in different ways. This is particularly true with respect to the effect of light. Light levels will not only affect the functional vision of individuals differently, but may also have a different effect according to the stage of a particular condition. Relevant design and specification requirements therefore aim to maximise flexibility and adjustability to enable a particular occupant to select conditions within their home to best suit their particular needs.

## 1.2 PREVALENCE OF SIGHT LOSS

The prevalence of sight loss increases with age. A Medical Research Council study[1] has estimated that serious sight loss (which would be registerable) affects:

- 1:8 of people aged over 75,

- 1:3 of people aged over 90.

Thus, using 2005 population data, this means that around 600,000 people over 75 years old suffer serious sight loss.

However, less serious sight loss can have a significant effect on the activities of daily living. It has been estimated that some 2 million people in the UK have sight loss that affects their everyday life. Given the normal ageing processes of the eye[2], most of the 13 million people in the UK over the age of 60 could benefit from better lighting at home. As the population ages, this figure will rise.

Few people with sight loss are totally blind. Most have some residual vision and appropriate design can help to maximise their functional vision.

## 1.3 FORMAT OF THIS GUIDE

Preceding the technical chapters in this *Guide* is a section discussing the general principles and considerations that designers need to be familiar with from the outset. These general principles and considerations are over-riding and inform the more detailed information contained within the technical chapters.

The technical chapters focus on functional areas or components and begin with a statement of primary objective. This is followed by:

- a list of design considerations to be borne in mind when working towards a design solution,

- a list of requirements that the final design and specification solution should achieve.

Considerations and requirements in this *Guide* may, at times, be repeated in different sections through the publication. This reflects the requirement for the *Guide* to be a practical reference tool for practitioners in housing development.

Five profiles that feature adults with sight loss, male and female, of all ages and with differing eye conditions are included at different points within the *Guide*. They demonstrate each individual's particular needs when it comes to their living arrangements. All these cases demonstrate the complexity of living with sight loss and particular design and specification requirements that need to be catered for, both in the overall design of the dwelling and its subsequent 'fine tuning' to suit each person. They also demonstrate the changing stages people go through depending on their life circumstances and the progression, of their vision impairment, and how potential for adjustment and adaptation within the dwelling will assist them to maintain their quality of life.

## 1.4 DESIGN BASIS AND STANDARDS

### 1.4.1 Inclusive design

This *Guide* promotes inclusive design based on the social model of disability which focuses on the design of the built environment not on an individual's impairment. An inclusive environment aims to assist use by everyone, regardless of age, gender or disability. It does not attempt to meet every single need, but by considering people's diversity it aims to break down unnecessary barriers and exclusion.

### 1.4.2 Lifetime Homes

The Lifetime Homes criteria act as the basic accessibility and adaptability standard throughout the *Guide*. In tune with the inclusive design approach, they aim to create environments with a built fabric that is accessible and adaptable to suit the needs of people with a range of mobility impairments.

The criteria are not readily apparent within the *Guide*. Where relevant, they are absorbed within the stated requirements, enabling the main focus to remain on the detailed design specification requirements relating to people with sight loss.

### 1.4.3 Scope

The inclusive design approach, Lifetime Homes and specific design for sight loss will not provide for every individual need. While Lifetime Homes criteria provide enhanced accessibility and adaptability to enable adjustments to suit reduced mobility, they will not achieve full wheelchair housing standards. Developers needing to achieve such standards should therefore cross-reference to other specialist guides (eg *Wheelchair housing design guide*[3]. Similarly, some Black and Minority Ethnic households may have specific requirements not covered by this *Guide* so additional guidance may be required. While some specification items in this *Guide* will also generally assist people with sensory impairments other than sight loss, further specialist guidance should be sought for environments relating to the needs of deaf and hearing-impaired people.

### 1.4.4 Statutory and legislative requirements

It is the duty of designers referring to this *Guide* to ensure that all statutory and legislative requirements are met in full on any development. Statutory and legislative requirements current at the time of development must take precedence over the requirements of this *Guide*.

# CHAPTER 2
# DESIGNING FOR PEOPLE WITH SIGHT LOSS

## 2.1 GENERAL PRINCIPLES AND CONSIDERATIONS

### 2.1.1 Inclusive design

The inclusive design principles outlined in *Chapter 1* should be incorporated throughout the requirements in this *Guide*.

Designers should ensure that their resulting design solutions do not immediately appear to be anything other than well-designed housing. The inclusive features and particular characteristics relating to designing for people with sight loss should be as inconspicuous as possible and not immediately apparent to sighted people. This is a fundamental design consideration and should be applied throughout the design process when meeting the requirements of this *Guide*. The resulting developments should therefore not appear to set accommodation for people with sight loss apart from mainstream accommodation.

### 2.1.2 Site location

Site location is another fundamental consideration. Independence, security, social inclusion and a sense of belonging (which have a significant effect on the quality of life for people with sight loss) are all affected by site location.

Site proximity to important amenities and good transport links, and the safe and relative ease of access to these facilities is key to enabling independence and social inclusion.

The presence of good local facilities is the optimum arrangement, enabling short travel distances within a local environment. Shopping, banking and leisure facilities should all, ideally, be available locally.

Local facilities and their use will, through familiarity, also provide a sense of neighbourhood and community which can reduce isolation and affect how safe people feel when moving around the area. When considering a site's location, the designer should consider whether a 'home patch' (an immediate neighbourhood offering day-to-day local facilities) can be readily identified.

Older people may be even more reliant on local facilities. Results of consultation show that the local facilities regarded as important to the majority of older people with sight loss are local (general) shops, a Post Office, a GP/health centre, a supermarket, a bank, a hairdresser, a dentist and a chemist. Other desirable facilities are recreational and social facilities and day-to-day service providers such as a newsagent, a chiropodist, a veterinary clinic and a dry cleaner.

Sites should be in a neighbourhood considered relatively safe and secure. The need for a secure neighbourhood is even more important for developments involving accommodation for older people (who may be frail and therefore more vulnerable).

Sites with excessive background traffic or other noise should be avoided. High levels of ambient noise can cause difficulty in orientation and concentration when leaving a quieter indoor home environment. The sense of safety in a neighbourhood can also be related to the amount of distracting information that needs to be processed and assessed. Busy neighbourhoods can lead to information overload and heighten the sense of vulnerability.

In addition to traffic noise, the quantity and speed of local traffic can pose difficulties for pedestrian movement away from the immediate home environment. Proximity of main roads, their relationship to routes to facilities, and the provision of safe crossing points should be considered. If necessary, liaise with the local Highways authority to seek or explore potential for improvements in relation to safe crossing points and controlled and audible crossings within the surrounding network of roads, particularly those on the route to the local facilities.

The availability and quality of the local transport should also be considered. Investigations should take place with the relevant organisations in respect of planned or potential for improvements to the local transport and transport stops. Improvements in stop locations, audible indicator boards, better visible destination boards, more accessible vehicles with on-board voice announcement of destinations and arrivals may be possible.

Details of discussions with the Highways department and transport providers, together with contact details should be passed to the client for ongoing liaison.

Where relevant, investigations of the Local Area Plan, Unitary Development Plan and discussions with the Local Authority's Planning Department should also be made to establish any known, forecast or predicted changes in a site's immediate location and local environment/'home patch'. Sites with significant planned changes to the existing pedestrian network to or from or within its local facilities should be discussed with the client to determine whether the advantages of the site, together with any advantages of the planned changes, outweigh the temporary difficulties caused by the building works themselves, followed by the need for people to re-learn the changed network of routes. Similarly, if sites are with, or adjacent to, an area of planned major works or a major maintenance programme, details of the work, its timescale/duration, noise disturbance and interruption to familiar routes should be determined and discussed with the client.

## 2.1.3 Site layout

Site layouts should be simple and logical.

Orientation of dwellings and their position in relation to other features (manmade and natural) should, as far as is practical, maximise the amount of natural daylight to the dwellings. However, appropriate means to avoid excessive solar gain, both in respect of overheating and as a potential source of glare, should be incorporated as necessary.

Orientation and layout should enable gardens and areas for external seating to have some direct sunlight for at least part of the year.

The pedestrian routes within the site should be simple, logical, clear and accessible with visual and sensory clues to aid orientation.

The designer should ensure that pedestrian routes on larger developments, once established at completion, will be permanent with no changes or disturbance. This means that there should be no alteration necessary to incorporate a neighbouring development or later phases of development, unless this would lead to significant long-term gain.

Very large, open, communal areas should not be included as these can be disorientating.

## 2.1.4 Mix and form of dwellings

As a general principle, funding organisations and developers who are enabling and providing the national stock of dwellings should seek to provide a broad portfolio that is suitable for the range of households having people with sight loss. There should be enough choice to cover the needs of different household types and sizes. The stock of dwellings following this design guidance should therefore be varied in scale, setting, form and tenure.

In the context of briefing designers, the client should determine the mix and preferred form of dwellings on each development, having regard to their objectives (or their clients' needs) and the overall aims for the development. The guidance contained in this publication is intended to be applicable and helpful to relevant design and specification details of the building, regardless of its type, scale, form, construction and general specification. It does not intend to discuss or inform housing need in relation to accommodation size, form, support, extra care or tenure. However, some general aspects do need to be considered and these are outlined below.

As a fundamental principle, housing provision should aim to integrate sectors of society as far as is practical and desirable to create inclusive societies. This will tend to promote interdependence and mutual support and reduce the isolation of people with disabilities, sensory or otherwise, from mainstream society. Developments following the principles of this *Guide* should have integration as a priority and should avoid, as far as is practical, setting people with impaired vision apart.

Whether or not a development will consist of or include supported housing, should be determined by the client. However, the form of any supported provision should be carefully considered and discussed with the client. Some studies show that the current typical model, seeking to cater for a wide range of tenants under one roof, can lead to service users feeling that support and management staff become overstretched, needing to focus on high-dependency tenants at the expense of those with equally important but lower levels of support needs. The form of provision of support for the range of tenants with differing support needs, when thoroughly discussed, may inform the physical nature of the development. It may, for example, be appropriate to form a 'cluster group' of higher supported provision integrated within the wider development, but offering distinct characteristics that promote increased mutual support and enable distinct staff management and support.

With the possible exception of supported housing, all dwellings should be designed as two-bedroom properties. One-bedroom properties or bedsits do not cater for guests or the need for occasional overnight care and support and can therefore increase isolation and dependency on alternative accommodation. One-bedroom properties may be feasible in supported housing if temporary guest accommodation is available nearby as part of the development. Bedsits, however, should not be provided within any part of any development, and any proposal for studio apartments with a defined sleeping area should be discussed and agreed with the client before inclusion.

The client, depending on the intended range of occupancy, will need to determine whether the dwellings are to be:

- completely self-contained and independent,

- independent and self-contained, but also having some communal areas and facilities, or

- independent but linked to wider communal and support facilities.

A larger development may contain a mix of the above options.

Clients may have additional specific design needs outside the scope of this *Guide*. People with sight loss from some Black and Minority Ethnic (BME) households may require larger accommodation enabling extended family arrangements or specific BME design and specification details relating to culture. Architects and designers may need to cross-reference other specialist guidance and ensure all relevant principles and requirements are included.

## 2.1.5 Space standards

Minimum space standards are not stated in this *Guide*. The requirements in each chapter should inform spatial arrangements. However, designers should ensure that adequate space to enable simple and direct circulation routes within all rooms and around the dwelling, clear of all obstacles and hazards, is provided. A furniture, fixture and fittings layout should be produced for each dwelling type detailing how this and the other requirements arising from the spatial considerations described below can be achieved for the given occupancy.

Rooms should not be an irregular shape and should be sensibly proportioned (eg long thin rooms should be avoided).

Some people may require the centre of living spaces to be completely free of obstacles and furniture. Wall space in living rooms should therefore be available for the required amount of furniture for the given occupancy. Practical furniture layouts should still be possible given this requirement and squarer rooms may enable this more readily.

Some people may have vision-assistive equipment in addition to the typical range of household items. This will require both additional storage facilities and sufficient table-top/work areas.

### 2.1.6 Simplicity

Simple, logical design of all external and internal layouts will assist orientation.

Simple, logical planning and layout will also tend to repeat the placing of certain features together in buildings (eg communal stairs adjacent to lifts), making them easier to find in unfamiliar buildings.

Simple and logical layouts also assist both the initial formation of a mental picture of the layout and the ability to remember this image. This may assist both the occupier in the early stages and also visitors with sight loss.

### 2.1.7 Consistency

Consistency of form and placing of specification items (eg switches and sockets at the same height and locations in rooms, door and window handles consistently located, hot and cold taps in the same form on the same sides, etc.) should be maximised. Their locations will therefore be easier to find and remember. This should be applied throughout each dwelling methodically and also across the entire development as far as is practical.

Variations on internal layout designs for the same occupancy levels should be minimised across a development. This will assist neighbours visiting other residents. 'Handing' dwellings of the same internal layout is acceptable where this is absolutely necessary to reduce potential noise disturbance through party walls. Where 'handing' is necessary, the approach taken should be consistently applied throughout a development.

The exception to the 'consistency rule' relates to external dwelling features which may act as way finding and location clues when moving around a development (eg varying front door colours, or gate/porch designs. This may assist residents in distinguishing one property from another — see Chapters 4 and 5.

### 2.1.8 Preventing barriers and trip hazards

Designers should locate everything out of the main line of pedestrian travel.

All ground surfaces on pedestrian routes should be even and remain so (ie not prone to differential movement, thus creating trip hazards).

Upstands (eg kerbs) should either be eliminated or conform to the specification given later in external requirements.

External steps and steep ramps should be designed out from the outset and/or conform to the requirements detailed in *Chapters 3* and *4*.

All thresholds should be level and eliminate trip hazards as detailed in *Chapter 5*.

### 2.1.9 Providing contrasts

While avoiding a garish appearance, providing bigger, bolder and brighter contrasts between adjacent surfaces, potential obstacles/hazards and their background, and controls and their background, is a general principle to be applied.

Careful selection of the overall colour and tonal scheme throughout each property and communal areas should avoid the appearance of anything other than a well-designed typical domestic environment. Sighted people should not immediately notice any specific difference in the development's design and specification. An institutional appearance or that of a care environment should be avoided.

Depth of contrast, ie lightness/darkness (within a similar colour palette or hue) can often be used effectively in place of two distinctly contrasting colours to avoid a garish appearance. The references to visual and colour contrasts throughout this *Guide* refer to differences in lightness/darkness of adjacent surfaces as opposed to two distinctly different hues. Sometimes, people with sight loss are unable to perceive the difference between two distinct colours of a similar lightness.

A discussion on contrast, its measurability, and effective provision, to which all references to 'contrast' in this *Guide* relate, is included in *Appendix A*.

Equipment and components supplied should have clear and accentuated indicators and controls. Indicators should have large numerals/symbols, and controls should be clear and prominent with tactile and audible clues (eg raised surfaces, switching with pre-set defined levels and audible clicks, etc.).

### 2.1.10 Textures and finishes

Large areas of highly polished/mirror-like reflective surfaces and finishes should be avoided whenever possible (across all items) as they may become a source of glare.

Finishes should generally be comfortable to the touch for people 'feeling' their way.

Designers should consider where textures can be used to provide assistive information, eg by varying the texture underfoot to provide a clue to location, including the presence of a feature or edge of a route. *Note:* the recognised range of tactile hazard pavings have distinct meanings according to the texture profile and should be used solely for the intended message. Tactile signage with Braille and embossed characters should also be used in accordance with the recommendations in the *Sign design guide*[4].

## 2.1.11 Wayfinding assistance

In the external environment or within communal internal settings, the use of colour (eg different front door/gate colours, different brick shades for different blocks of housing, colour themes for different storeys in communal corridors) can assist in wayfinding or determining location.

Similarly, the use of different designs (eg varying the form of front gates) can provide the same assistance.

Well-placed, distinctive and scented plants, and the siting of street furniture can also be used as navigation aids and offer wayfinding assistance.

## 2.1.12 Lighting

Lighting is discussed in detail in *Chapter 14* and throughout the functional chapters in this *Guide*. However, the following basic principles are worth noting from the outset.

Good and consistent levels of lighting are required throughout the development both externally and internally.

Natural light levels should be maximised, particularly in task locations such as kitchens.

All light sources, whether natural or artificial, are a potential source of glare. Artificial lighting lamps should always be fully shielded or diffused from the user's full range of possible sight lines, and natural light sources should have the potential to be fully obscured with blinds.

Design and specification should enable adjustability and tailoring of light levels for all tasks and movement within each dwelling to suit the varying needs of individuals. The various eye conditions (see *Chapter 1*) affect the reaction of people with sight loss to lights and lighting in different ways. The effect light has on functional vision may also vary according to the stage of a particular condition. No two people will be affected in the same way by lighting levels and light sources and different occupants within the same dwelling may also need to adjust the lighting provision to their own individual needs.

It is therefore of paramount importance to maximise flexibility and controllability by providing a range of internal lighting fittings (and ample sockets for portable task lighting within each dwelling) which will enable each occupant to achieve their own particular optimum lighting levels.

Throughout this *Guide*, the principle is applied that increased lighting levels will enable people with sight loss to maximise use of their remaining functional vision. However, some people will find even normal levels of light uncomfortably bright or disabling so the *Guide* therefore also includes appropriate design and specification requirements to counteract negative effects of normal lighting levels when needed.

### 2.1.13 Security

Security is particularly important for those who may be perceived as vulnerable. It is also important to ensure that the design and specification items included enable them to feel safe and secure, both within their individual dwellings and when moving around internal and external communal areas. *Secured by design*[5] certification is required for every development to ensure that crime deterrence is incorporated in accordance with the advice of the relevant local practitioners and directly related to the needs and characteristics of each particular site and neighbourhood. In addition, particular security specification items regarding the specific needs of people with sight loss, are discussed in the relevant chapters, regardless of the *Secured by design*[5] specification.

## *Profile 1:* Additional assistive equipment needs more space

**For Jim, a self-employed middle-aged man, being blind from birth has not restricted his movements or made him dependent on others. He has lived on his own in the same flat for 20 years, with adaptations and adjustments to the design to accommodate his lack of vision.**

Jim has retinopathy of prematurity (ROP) and an inoperable cataract in the left eye. He was able to see some colour contrast until the age of 18, when his functional vision was reduced to some recognition of light and dark only. While Jim's level of vision is constant, he sees marginally more in the spring and summer because the sunlight is brighter. He is unable to see electric lighting, only natural light through windows.

*'I lived in a hostel specifically for people with sight loss, but outgrew it because everything was done for me.'*

Jim's current rented one-bed flat was formerly a bedsit with shared facilities (often with unsuitable co-tenants), but all units in the block have now been made self-contained. Jim receives only minimal practical assistance: a cleaner once a week and an on-site handyman who is available to assist any tenant in the block.

Key assistive equipment in the flat includes:
• Braille encryption equipment,
• a digital radio and alarm clock with speaking function, and
• a Braille microwave.

Other helpful equipment includes:
• a laptop, and
• a note-taker.

All this equipment requires adequate surface space without compromising space for other typical household items. Knowing where these things are, and not having to move them around or change their position is important in enabling Jim's independence.

*'My flat's location in London is a big bonus because of the excellent transport links.'*

There is a Tube station close to Jim's flat and another only a short distance away, giving access to a number of different Tube lines. The voice announcements on the Tube trains and platforms are very helpful.

Although currently a tenant, Jim is interested in shared ownership options and would like the opportunity to buy, or part-buy, a suitable property.

# TECHNICAL GUIDANCE

# SECTION 1
## External areas

# CHAPTER 3
# PUBLIC AND COMMUNAL AREAS OUTSIDE PLOT BOUNDARIES

### 3.1 PRINCIPLE

- **Minimise hazards and provide a high degree of accessibility within the development.**

### 3.2 DESIGN CONSIDERATIONS

Estate roads and footpaths should follow simple and logical layouts.

Adoption of communal areas and services by the local authority and utility providers should be maximised. Standards for adoption should be assessed against the principles and requirements within this *Guide* and any discrepancies discussed with the relevant authority to seek agreement to necessary revisions.

The provision of wayfinding clues such as distinctive and scented planting, the siting of street furniture, etc., can assist orientation around large developments, particularly those with repetitive street patterns.

The pedestrian network should be accessible. Gradients on footpaths should be eliminated or reduced as far as possible. Layouts wherever feasible should enable footpath routes with gradients not exceeding 1:12.

Shared surfaces (eg pedestrian/cycle paths) are potentially dangerous for people with sight loss and should not be provided.

Open spaces, squares, etc. with no constant guiding features above ground level can be disorientating and should not be incorporated into the layout.

Designers should ensure that the lighting scheme proposed for adoption will provide an even and constant level of lighting for all areas after dusk. Additional lighting above the minimum standard for adoption may be required to achieve this. Designers should also have regard for the Institution of Lighting Engineers' *Guidance notes for the reduction of obtrusive light*[6] to reduce the potential for light pollution.

The placing of every item of street furniture should be considered carefully as each is potentially a hazard.

Clear delineation between private and public boundaries throughout the development will assist in wayfinding and general movement around the development.

## 3.3 REQUIREMENTS

### 3.3.1 Footpaths/ pavements

#### 3.3.1.1 Obstructions and hazards

All footpaths should have a clear minimum width of 1200 mm free of obstacles and obstructions.

Where necessary, measures such as kerb lines or bollards (placed beyond the edge of the path) should be incorporated to prevent parked cars from overhanging the footpath and bikes/cars from parking on the footpath.

Low-level planting, unless contained behind a wall of minimum height 300 mm, should not be provided adjacent to footpaths as this may become a trip hazard by growing over the footpath.

Other planting adjacent to or close to footpaths should be positioned to prevent it, when mature, from becoming a hazard by growing out over the edge of the footpath line or by overhanging the footpath. Overhanging trees can be both an obstruction hazard and a slip hazard due to leaf fall (Figure 1).

Bin stores should be positioned so that they, or any associated doors that are left open, do not infringe the footpath.

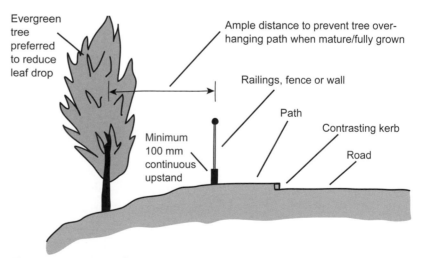

*Figure 1:* Section showing requirements for footpaths/pavements where land falls away

*Note* upstand and barrier to the back edge of the path, also tree choice and position to prevent overhanging and leaf drop to footpath.

**(a)** Pedestrian routes should have a clear height of 2250 mm from the ground for the entire width of the footpath

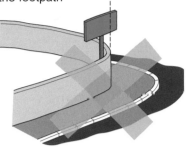

**(b)** Tree positioned to prevent it overhanging the footpath when fully grown. Evergreen, fragrant, or distinctively shaped planting is preferred

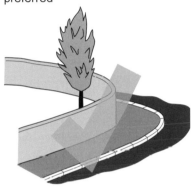

*Figure 2:* Natural and manmade features should be placed to assist wayfinding and orientation but should not become an obstacle hazard

Gates to gardens, where provided, should open inwards.

All street furniture should be recessed off the footpath/circulation route. There should not be any signage or protrusions from street furniture over the footpath that are less than 2250 mm above the path (Figure 2).

Designers should ensure that any advertising sign board, projecting pavement display, awning, sign, etc., from any commercial premises within the development is clear of the edges of the pavement for a height of 2250 mm above the ground.

### 3.3.1.2 Surfaces
Surfaces should be smooth, even and slip-resistant.

Continuous materials are preferred to reduce the risk of trip hazards in the future. Flag stones/paving stones/brick paviors, etc. increase the risk of trip hazards and disruption due to differential settlement and subsequent maintenance. Designers should have due regard for the compaction and potential settlement of the ground if incorporating surface finishes with joints.

### 3.3.1.3 Kerbs/footpath edges
All footpath edges should have a distinct vertical boundary or kerb.

All footpath edges not abutting a vertical wall or boundary should be clearly distinguished from adjacent roads and all other surfaces by clear kerb lines that contrast in colour with the adjacent surface.

Generally, the kerbs should be flush with the footpath surface and contrast to its texture.

Where the ground surface adjacent to the footpath is at a significantly different level or involves a sudden change in level, a kerb upstand should be provided. The upstand should be a minimum height of 100 mm and be accompanied by a handrail (Figure 1).

The height of kerbs from road surfaces should be consistent throughout the development (excluding dropped kerb locations). Shallow kerb upstands which may be a trip hazard should not be included. Dropped kerbs should be flush, or have a chamfered profile not exceeding 15 mm in height.

### 3.3.1.4 Gradients
Site planning and layout should seek to minimise gradients on all paths and especially on those approaching buildings.

Level or minimal gradients should be the aim. Where this is not possible, slopes rather than steps are required. The gradients of slopes should not exceed 1:12. Steps should only be included where it is not possible to provide reasonable routes that conform to the maximum gradient requirements of 1:12. Where steps need to be incorporated to enable a reasonable route, an alternative footpath route, without steps or gradients exceeding 1:12, should be provided. Developments containing accommodation for wheelchair users should conform to the slope gradient/maximum distance requirements of the *Wheelchair housing design guide*[3].

Steps, where unavoidable, should have colour-contrasting nosings extending the full width of every step. The nosings should be between 50 mm and 65 mm in depth and should be flush with the step's tread and riser. All steps should be consistent in form with treads that are no less than 280 mm and risers that do not exceed 150 mm. Handrails are required to both sides of any steps together with an upstand kerb of between 100 and 200 mm in height. All steps (but not ramps) should have tactile warning (see section on *Hazard pavings* below). All steps should be enclosed below to prevent people from walking into their underside and to provide vertical surfaces for guidance.

Crossfalls should be minimised to that necessary for effective drainage.

### 3.3.1.5 Tactile hazard pavings

Hazard pavings should be incorporated into communal areas, but only at correct locations and ensuring the correct surface pattern for the location. Each surface pattern, and sometimes its positioning in relation to the feature it is highlighting, has a distinct meaning. Their use should be in accordance with the latest Department of Transport guidance[7].

*Modified blister paving* (small, regular flat-topped domes) should be used to alert pedestrians to a designated crossing point (Pelican or Zebra crossing) and/or to warn that the kerb has been dropped to assist those with impaired mobility.

*Hazard-warning paving* (corduroy: half-rod-shaped bars) should be used to give warning of a hazard which requires caution (eg at the top and bottom of steps).

*Directional guidance paving* (round-ended bars are used to guide people through large open spaces (eg a town square), the bars being laid in the direction of travel and turned at corners. However, such large open spaces tend to relate to urban planning rather than smaller-scale environments. Large open spaces can be disorientating so they should be avoided on housing developments.

### 3.3.1.6 Drainage gratings and inspection chamber covers

Whenever possible, drainage gratings and inspection chamber covers should be located off footpaths as wear and tear and differential settlement may cause them to become a trip hazard. Maintenance and cleaning work may also cause temporary obstacles.

When this is not practical, they should be set out of the main line of travel and flush with the surrounding surface. The grill lines should be perpendicular to the direction of travel (to minimise the risk of canes or wheelchair wheels being disturbed or trapped).

No opening in a grill or grating should exceed 13 mm in width.

## 3.3.2 Street furniture

All street furniture should be sited to assist orientation by providing 'landmarks' and 'signposts'. However, it should not be sited within the range of pedestrian directional travel on any footpath where it may be an obstacle hazard.

All street furniture should contrast against its background.

Posts/columns, as well as contrasting with their background, should have a further white or light-coloured band 150 mm wide at typical eye level and be between 1400 mm and 1600 mm from the ground.

Bollards, where provided, should not be linked by chains or ropes. They should contrast against their background and have a further contrasting band at their neck (close to their top). They should have a minimum height of 1000 mm. They should not have any protrusions.

Any furniture or signage protruding from posts should be above 2250 mm from the ground (ie above head height) or should not protrude over the footpath.

Signs where provided should be in accordance with recommendations within the *Sign design guide*[4].

## 3.3.3 Planting

Where incorporated, planting should be chosen to assist in wayfinding by a distinct shape, colour, aroma or texture. It should be chosen and located whenever possible to provide directional 'signposts' or 'landmarks'.

All planting areas should be located or designed to prevent growth over footpaths, whether direct or overhanging. The size of the plants when mature should be considered.

Evergreen, rather than deciduous, trees are preferred as fallen leaves can create a slip hazard.

Slow-growing and low-maintenance plants should be used whenever possible as these will help to reduce potential hazards.

Dense low-level ground-cover planting will deter litter from gathering around it and also discourage weed growth.

Unless a feature plant is used to assist with wayfinding, all planting should be sufficiently low level to avoid creating 'hiding places' for unsocial activity or prospective attackers/ intruders.

### 3.3.4 Parking

Overall parking provision, whether private, semi-private or communal should be sufficient to prevent vehicles parking in undesignated spaces, especially with wheels on footpaths.

Any provision 'end on' to footpaths should incorporate features such as bollards, set off the footpath, or wheel stops, to prevent cars overhanging the footpath. Ensure any such provision is located off the line of pedestrian travel and detailed to prevent it being a trip hazard or obstacle.

Blocks of flats without parking/vehicle access within their site boundary should be provided with a convenient pick-up/drop-off point close to the main entrance.

### 3.3.5 Lighting

The lighting scheme should achieve a good level of consistent light around all pedestrian routes and communal areas after dusk.

The scheme should avoid dimly lit corners.

The scheme, while achieving the lighting objectives, should also have regard to the reduction or elimination of obtrusive light and light pollution. Guidance notes are available from the Institution of Lighting Engineers[6].

### 3.3.6 Colour contrasts

Footpath surfaces should contrast against adjacent walls, an adjacent road or other ground surfaces.

Kerbs should contrast with the footpath surface.

Nosings on any steps should contrast against the steps.

# CHAPTER 4
# PRIVATE AREAS WITHIN PLOT BOUNDARIES FOR HOUSES OR BLOCKS OF FLATS

**4.1 PRINCIPLE**

- **Ensure that spaces within the plot boundaries of the home minimise hazards and provide a usable environment.**

**4.2 DESIGN CONSIDERATIONS**

Parking and path layout within dwelling/block curtilages should be simple and logical. Parking should be close to the main entrance.

Front gardens with a clear boundary between the garden and the street are the preferred method for defining the boundary between public and private/semi-private spaces.

Studies conducted for Thomas Pocklington Trust by Professor Julienne Hanson and colleagues show that around 1/3 of older people with sight loss consider a garden/open space as 'essential' with 70% regarding it as a 'desirable' or 'important' feature.

All paths should be fully accessible, level or gently sloping, and barrier-free.

Main access paths should be easily distinguishable both during daylight and after dusk.

Access routes and shared communal areas should be well-lit and evenly lit after dusk and other routes around the dwelling should contain lighting to deter intruders. There is some evidence that the white light from, for example metal halide or fluorescent lamps, is more effective than the more orange light from sodium lamps.

## 4.3 REQUIREMENTS

**4.3.1 General**

As far as practicable, access to a garden or private/semi-private outdoor space should be provided for every dwelling.

Dwellings at ground-floor level, according to designed occupancy, should either have a private and secure garden (family dwellings) or patio area. Back gardens should meet the *Secured by design*[5] specification with regards to access and boundary treatments. Private back gardens to individual properties should contain a level patio area of minimum 2400 × 1800 mm and clothes-drying facilities accessed from a patio or path.

Flats above the ground floor should, whenever possible, be designed with a private and secure balcony.

In addition, flatted developments, whenever possible, should have a secure communal garden accessible to all residents (see *Chapter 16*).

### 4.3.2 Paths

Communal paths should maintain a minimum clear width of 1200 mm. A wider width may be desirable. There should be no obstacles within this clear width for the duration of the path (Figure 3).

Paths serving individual dwellings should maintain a clear width of 900 mm. There should be no obstacles within this clear width for the duration of the path.

All entrance paths from the street and car-parking spaces should be level or gently sloping. Ideally, the paths should be level. Where topography prevents level paths, an individual slope of less than 5 m may have a maximum gradient of 1:12, a single slope of between 5 and 10 m may have a maximum gradient of 1:15. Level resting areas of at least 1200 mm in length should be provided at the top and bottom of such individual slopes. A slope in excess of 10 m in length should have a maximum gradient not exceeding 1:20.

Parking should be close to the main entrance, enabling a short simple route to the entrance.

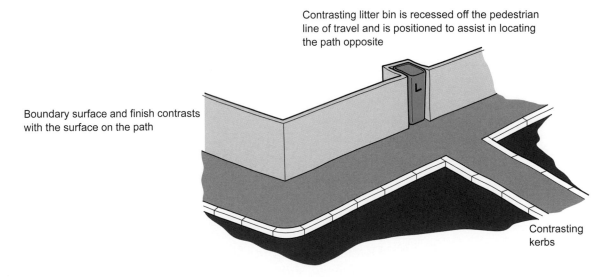

Contrasting litter bin is recessed off the pedestrian line of travel and is positioned to assist in locating the path opposite

Boundary surface and finish contrasts with the surface on the path

Contrasting kerbs

*Figure 3:* Street furniture should be placed to prevent obstacle hazards and act as wayfinding clues

Where necessary, measures such as additional kerb lines or bollards (placed beyond the edge of the path) should be incorporated to prevent parked cars from overhanging the footpath and bikes/cars from parking on the footpath.

Low-level planting unless contained behind a wall of a minimum height of 300 mm, should not be provided adjacent to footpaths as this may become a trip hazard by growing over the path.

Other landscaping adjacent to or close to paths should be positioned to prevent it, when mature, from becoming a hazard by growing out over the edge of the path, or overhanging the footpath which may be both an obstruction hazard and a slip hazard from fallen leaves.

Distinctively shaped, coloured or fragrant plants should be considered to assist in wayfinding by their strategic location.

Bin stores and other stores should be positioned so that they, or any associated doors that are left open, do not infringe the path.

All path surfaces should be smooth, even and slip-resistant when both wet and dry.

Continuous materials are preferred to reduce the potential for trip hazards from differential settlement and subsequent disruption due to maintenance. Flag stones/paving stones/ brick paviors, etc. should not be used unless designers are confident that adequate specification can eliminate any potential for settlement.

All path edges should have a distinct vertical boundary or kerb (Figure 3).

All path edges not abutting a vertical wall or boundary should be clearly distinguished from adjacent surfaces by clear kerb lines that contrast in colour.

Generally, the kerbs should be flush with the path surface and contrast with its texture.

Where the ground surface adjacent to the path is at a different level (excluding driveways/parking spaces), a kerb upstand should be provided. The upstand should be a minimum height of 100 mm and accompanied by a handrail.

All paths should follow logical, simple routes and provide access to all facilities.

## 4.3.3 Dog runs

Flatted developments with communal external spaces should incorporate an enclosed and gated dog run where guide dogs can be taken for toileting. A smooth concreted floor is required with gradual falls to a foul drain with an easily removable cover. An external tap and hose is required to enable the area to be cleaned and washed away via the foul drain. The area for the run should be a minimum of 2000 × 2000 mm, though a longer run of at least 4000 mm long × 2000 mm wide is desirable.

Where private gardens have sufficient space to provide a dog run, a drain connection to a foul sewer and an external tap should be provided to enable easy provision of a run (by installation of the floor and enclosure) if and when required. The area for the future run should be a minimum 2000 × 2000 mm, though a longer run is desirable.

## 4.3.4 Car parking

Car parking provision should have regard to designed occupancy. It should always be located close to a principal entrance with a direct path link as detailed in the earlier section on *Paths* and in Figure 13.

Car parking spaces provided to individual dwellings should, in addition, also be capable of attaining a clear width of 3300 mm (possibly by locating a 900 mm path adjacent to a 2400 mm wide parking space).

## 4.3.5 Boundary treatments

### 4.3.5.1 General
Clear delineation of private or semi-private space with public space is required at all plot boundaries by the use of walls, fences or railings, and gates.

All boundary treatments not of continuous solid material (eg railings and some fences) should have a continuous solid upstand of at least 100 mm at ground level following the line of the boundary.

### 4.3.5.2 Front boundaries and gates
Clear boundaries, brick/stone walls, fencing or railings, all with gates, are required.

A minimum height of 800 mm is required.

Designers should consider assisting wayfinding by varying the form of gates and boundary treatments between properties where relevant.

Gates to access paths should have the dwelling numbers attached to them. Numerals should be tactile and contrast with their background. They should have a minimum height of 90 mm. Gates should open inwards and be prevented from opening outwards over the public footpath.

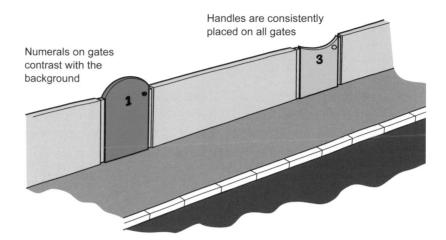

Handles are consistently
placed on all gates

Numerals on gates
contrast with the
background

Gates contrast with adjacent surfaces
and have clear numerals and varying
form to assist in locating each property

*Figure 4:* Varying form can assist wayfinding

They should have a simple automatic closing device. All pedestrian gates should have a minimum clear opening width of 800 mm with ironmongery no higher than 1200 mm from the ground.

### 4.3.5.3 Boundary treatments rear and side
Secure boundaries and gates to *Secured by design*[5] specifications are required. All pedestrian gates should have a minimum clear opening width of 800 mm with ironmongery no higher than 1200 mm from the ground.

### 4.3.6 Colour contrasts
Paths should contrast in colour and texture with their adjacent surfaces when both wet and dry.

Gates should contrast with the boundary treatments in which they are set (Figure 4).

Gates to different properties should vary in colour and/or form (Figure 4).

Numerals on gates should contrast against their background (Figure 4).

### 4.3.7 Lighting
Designers should ensure that a good consistent level of lighting on all entrance paths is provided after dark. This should achieve 50 lux on the pathway and sufficient light at head height to assist in the recognition of individuals while avoiding light pollution. The level of illuminance should increase in the porch area to provide a level of 200 lux vertically on the keyhole or face of equivalent control(s).

Pathways on pedestrian routes to the entrance, or other communal routes/areas that may be used after dusk, should be lit by fittings that do not emit light above the horizontal to provide light onto the path surface without glare (ie providing down lighting, generally). This provision should avoid light and dark patches and the fittings should be sited so that they are neither obstacles on the paths nor disruptive to wayfinding by feel or the use of canes.

Side paths and rear garden paths/areas serving individual private dwellings should be provided with sensor-activated security lighting that also provides an audible signal inside the home.

Dog runs need to be lit with lighting that is completely diffused to prevent it causing glare.

Private balconies should be lit with a ceiling luminaire or similar achieving suitable weather resistance (IP rating). These should be provided with suitable diffusers to prevent glare and should be individually switched from the inside.

# SECTION 2
## Functional spaces

# CHAPTER 5
# ENTRANCES TO
# INDIVIDUAL DWELLINGS

**5.1 PRINCIPLE**
- **Maximise the potential for visual clarity in the recognition and use of the entrance together with a high level of security.**

**5.2 DESIGN CONSIDERATIONS**

Providing variety (eg different door colours or porch design) at the entrances to similar or adjacent properties on a development, particularly a terrace or corridor, can assist in wayfinding and in distinguishing the approach to one property from another.

Natural daylight levels within the dwelling should be enhanced as far as practicable around the front door by maximising the amount of glazing. However, the designer should consider the possible need to provide blinds to counteract glare if required. These blinds will also assist in providing privacy and a greater sense of security.

Glazing provision within the door design and adjacent casements should take account of the potential hazard of full-height glazing.

The conflicting requirements for both privacy and visitor recognition without opening the door will need to be satisfied.

Movement in and around the confines of an entrance, often while welcoming visitors, can increase the risk of tripping. Threshold and mat well details should ensure level detailing to minimise the potential risk of falls.

For people with little or no vision, providing textural clues (eg by varying the ground surface texture and tone immediately outside the door) can assist in locating the door, accessing locks, etc.

Adequate lighting provision at the entrance door to enable identification of features, key finding and general security is an essential requirement.

Some degree of weather protection at external doors is required to provide some shelter for key location, opening the door and gaining access which may take longer for a person with sight loss.

The form of door, frame and adjacent surface should enable the easy installation of electronic devices to enable audible recognition of callers if required. See *Chapter 13, section on Door entry systems.*

Locking mechanisms to entrance doors should provide good security while being easy to operate by residents. Electronic key fobbing to individual dwelling doors within a secure communal internal setting may be appropriate if security is not compromised.

## 5.3 REQUIREMENTS

### 5.3.1 General

Where appropriate, vary the colour or style of doors or entrances along a terrace or corridor to assist in wayfinding and in distinguishing one property from another.

Maximise potential for natural light inside the entrance but ensure full-height glazing is avoided by the use of transoms.

Glazing should ensure that privacy can be maintained.

A means of caller recognition without opening the door should be provided, such as an area of clear glazing or a door viewer. In addition, the potential need for a system enabling audible caller recognition or a door-entry system should be discussed and determined with the client.

The designer should ensure that the ironmongery and general design of the door, adjacent casements, etc. would not prevent all glazing from being fully obscured with blinds (to prevent glare and to provide security) if required.

A nominally level area of at least 1200 × 1200 mm should be provided outside every entrance door. Where this is external, it should contrast in tonal colour and texture with the entrance path/surrounding surfaces.

External entrance doors should be provided with some degree of shelter from the weather. The minimum requirement is for a canopy 1200 mm wide × 800 mm deep. Any support posts and/or brackets should not be an obstacle to circulation or potential hazard to people's heads.

### 5.3.2 Thresholds and mat wells

Designers should seek to eliminate all trip hazards. All thresholds should be level and where door mats are necessary these should be set into mat wells so that the finished surface of the mat is level with the surrounding floor. Door mats and their mat wells should be standard off-the-peg and easily replaceable sizes. Any mats should be robust, and resistant to wear and fraying.

### 5.3.3 Effective clear opening width

All entrance doors to individual dwellings should have a minimum effective clear opening width of 800 mm.

### 5.3.4 Ironmongery

All ironmongery should colour contrast against the door surface.

All ironmongery should be easy and comfortable to 'feel' and operate. Door handles should be lever-type or 'D'-type according to locking/latch arrangements. The type should be consistent and set at a consistent height throughout the entire development.

Ironmongery should meet the above requirements without giving any appearance other than that of a typical domestic environment.

Locking mechanisms should meet *Secured by design*[5] requirements.

The letter box should be centred within the door with an internal letter cage to the inside of the front door. Sufficient clearance to any side wall should be provided to enable the door to open to a full 90° with the letter cage in place.

Door numerals (in addition to those sited on any gates) should be fixed at a constant height and located on, or immediately adjacent to, the doors throughout the development. They should contrast against their background and range between 90–150 mm in height according to the distance at which they will need to be read.

### 5.3.5 Lighting

External lighting should be connected to 'dusk to dawn' light level sensors to give automatic night-day activation, and activation when dim light occurs during daylight hours. It should be located to give an even level of light, achieving 200 lux vertically on the lock or face of an equivalent mechanism, at the front door area.

The lighting should illuminate all the features and facilities connected with the entrance including the key hole.

Glare should be avoided to those entering or leaving the dwelling. Unshielded bulkhead luminaires should not be used.

Conduit and capped-off electrical supplies should be installed to enable the future provision of additional lighting connected to a PIR movement detector that is capable of providing an internal audible signal when activated.

### 5.3.6 Finishes and colour contrasts

The colour finish on each door should contrast against the adjacent wall surface. It should not be a high gloss finish.

A range of colour finishes on doors should be used so that dwellings adjacent to each other have different door colours.

Glazing should, wherever possible, incorporate transoms (ie not be full height). Any full-height glazing at eye level should incorporate a distinctive, but unfussy, band or motif, minimum of 150 mm square, between 1400 and 1600 mm from the floor.

All ironmongery, numerals, etc. should contrast against the door finish and be a non-reflective/non-glossy finish.

# CHAPTER 6
# HALLWAYS AND CIRCULATION AREAS WITHIN DWELLINGS

**6.1 PRINCIPLE**

- **Provide clear, simple circulation routes with features to assist navigation and safe movement.**

**6.2 DESIGN CONSIDERATIONS**

Hallways and circulation routes should be as short, as direct, and as simple as possible.

Clear widths of corridors and their associated doors should enable access to people with different degrees of mobility. The clear effective width of door openings should be consistent throughout the dwelling. The minimum clear effective width of internal doorways will therefore depend on the narrowest hallway passage/corridor adjacent to a door in accordance with the requirements below (see *General accessibility* below).

All doors on the entrance level should contain a short nib to the leading edge (eg a short length of wall in line with the closed door) to prevent the leading edge being tight into the corner of any room (Figure 5).

Potential obstacles on any circulation route should be designed out. Doors should not open out into hallways. Storage cupboards, whenever practicable, should have sliding doors. Pram and bike storage or wheelchair charging areas, where provided, should be recessed off routes. Ground-floor dwellings with private rear gardens should include an identified area for a guide dog to sleep. While this area need not necessarily be in the hallway, it should not interrupt or impede any circulation route/task area.

Turns of direction in hallways should preferably be 90°. A change of direction involving curves or oblique angles should be avoided wherever possible.

Stairs within a typical domestic environment generally record poor levels of both natural and artificial light. This, combined with the nature of circulation, creates a significant hazard which designers should address by lighting design. Finding the stair edges, handrails, and movement up and down the stairs will all need to be considered.

300 mm clear of any obstruction to assist those using mobility aids or wheelchairs when opening the door

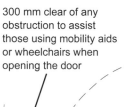
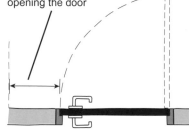

*Figure 5:* 300 mm door nib requirement to the leading edge of all doors on the entrance level of a dwelling and all communal doors

*Note:* Communal doors also require a 200 mm door nib on the push side

Generous storage space should be available within each dwelling, the majority of which should be accessed off the hallway. As well as storage requirements typical of the household size, additional storage should be provided to accommodate low vision equipment, assistive technology and additional support aids. It is important that adequate storage is available to prevent a cluttered and therefore hazardous dwelling.

Storage cupboards should be designed and located so that doors will not impede circulation routes when left open. Sliding doors on good quality mechanisms may be an option. Storage cupboard doors should conform to the requirements in sections 6.3.2, 6.3.3 and 6.3.4 below.

Internal lighting to all storage cupboards should be provided to assist in locating objects within the cupboard. Internal walls, shelves, etc. should have a matt finish, in a light colour, so that objects contrast against them.

Colour contrast should assist in locating all doorways off the hall, the stairs, and all ironmongery and controls.

## 6.3 REQUIREMENTS

### 6.3.1 General accessibility

Effective clear door widths should be consistent throughout the property and will relate to the minimum corridor/landing width approaching a door as detailed in Table 1.

The minimum hallway/landing width should be a clear 900 mm. However, 1050 mm or 1200 mm is preferred.

Radiators/other heaters should be positioned so that they do not become an obstacle hazard on a length of wall between two doorways.

| Table 1: Effective clear door widths | |
|---|---|
| **Minimum hallway/landing width at any point in the dwelling adjacent to a door (mm)** | **Corresponding minimum clear effective width for all internal doorways (to be applied consistently throughout the dwelling) (mm)** |
| 900 | 900 |
| 1050 | 775 |
| 1200 (or greater) | 750 |

*Note:* All doors on the entrance level should have a nib, 300 mm or longer, to the leading edge of the door, on the pull side (Figure 5).

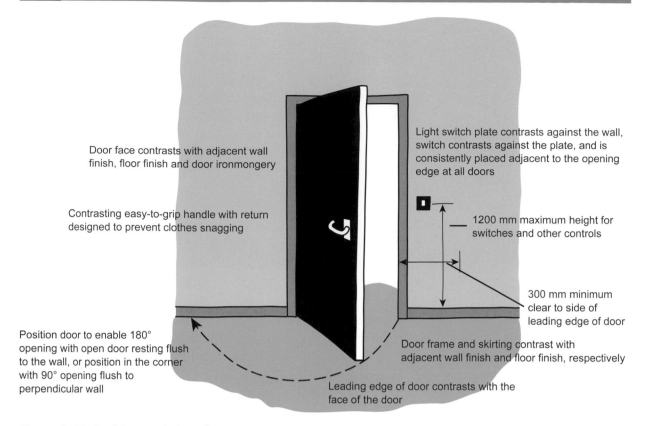

Light switch plate contrasts against the wall, switch contrasts against the plate, and is consistently placed adjacent to the opening edge at all doors

Door face contrasts with adjacent wall finish, floor finish and door ironmongery

Contrasting easy-to-grip handle with return designed to prevent clothes snagging

1200 mm maximum height for switches and other controls

300 mm minimum clear to side of leading edge of door

Position door to enable 180° opening with open door resting flush to the wall, or position in the corner with 90° opening flush to perpendicular wall

Door frame and skirting contrast with adjacent wall finish and floor finish, respectively

Leading edge of door contrasts with the face of the door

*Figure 6:* Typical internal door features

### 6.3.2 Internal doors

Internal doors should be:

- sliding, or

- hinged to open into a room and rest with the leading edge against an adjacent wall, or

- self-closing.

The opening method should be consistent throughout the property.

Ensure adequate clearance to side walls to enable all doors to open a full 90°, with allowance for all ironmongery including letter cages on the front door.

Where possible and practical given other design considerations, the hanging of doors to rooms should also be consistent throughout the dwelling so they are hinged on the same side.

Doors with no glazing are the preferred option. Where glazing is provided, large glazing panels should be avoided. Any glazing should incorporate a distinctive band or motif at eye level, and should be of toughened glass.

### 6.3.3 Internal door ironmongery

All ironmongery should contrast against the door surface (Figure 6).

All ironmongery should be easy and comfortable to 'feel' and operate.

Door handles on doors to rooms should be lever-type, with returns on the open edge to prevent clothing and other items from snagging on the handle (Figure 6).

All door handles should be at a consistent height throughout the entire development.

## 6.3.4 Internal door finishes and contrasts

Door and door frame colours should be a matt or satin finish, and give good colour contrast against their adjacent wall surfaces (Figure 6).

The leading edge of the door should also contrast against the general door colour (Figure 6).

## 6.3.5 Stairs within individual dwellings

Open stair risers are dangerous and should not be provided in any situation.

Stairs should be enclosed below to prevent people from walking into their underside.

Adequate risers and goings are required. Maximum height of a riser should be 170 mm, minimum length of a going should be 250 mm (Figure 7).

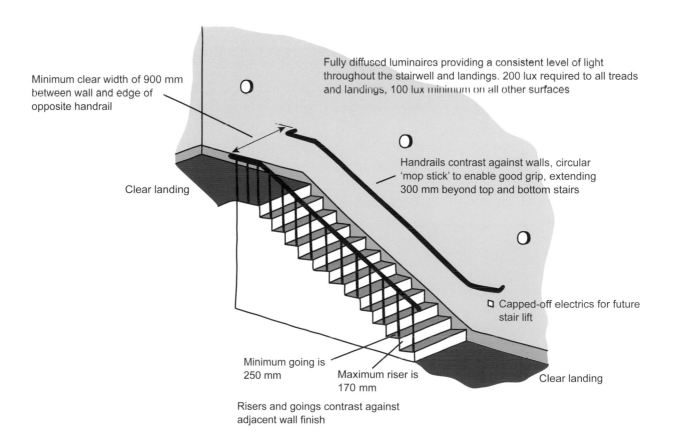

Minimum clear width of 900 mm between wall and edge of opposite handrail

Fully diffused luminaires providing a consistent level of light throughout the stairwell and landings. 200 lux required to all treads and landings, 100 lux minimum on all other surfaces

Clear landing

Handrails contrast against walls, circular 'mop stick' to enable good grip, extending 300 mm beyond top and bottom stairs

Capped-off electrics for future stair lift

Minimum going is 250 mm

Maximum riser is 170 mm

Clear landing

Risers and goings contrast against adjacent wall finish

*Figure 7:* Typical details for a domestic stair in an individual dwelling

Stairs should maintain a clear width of 900 mm from one wall (behind the handrail) to the edge of the opposing handrail (Figure 7).

Straight flights are preferred. Level landings are required at any turn. Winders should not be included on stairs.

Continuous circular 'mop stick' handrails, well secured and with adequate clearance for firm grip between the rail and the wall, are required on both sides of the stair. When against a wall, these should extend for 300 mm beyond the top and bottom stair (Figure 7).

A domestic stair should have capped-off electrics for the provision of a future stair lift (Figure 7).

### 6.3.6 Stair contrasts and finishes

The stair goings and risers should contrast with the adjacent walls.

Reflective materials that may cause glare should not be used at any point or for any component on the stair or stair finish.

Polished surfaces or other slippery surfaces should not be incorporated into the finish.

Tactile warnings should be provided at the top of the stairs in any communal setting but not necessarily at the top of stairs within individual private dwellings. The application should be consistent throughout the entire development.

The handrails should contrast in colour against the wall on which they are fixed.

Walls around the stairs should be painted in a light matt colour to maximise lighting levels.

### 6.3.7 Stair lighting

Good lighting is essential on all stairs and throughout the stairwell. It can significantly reduce the risk of accidents. Light sources should be positioned to maximise light flow throughout the stairwell.

While natural light should be maximised, windows in the vicinity of stairs should be fitted with effective blinds (see *Chapter 11*). Windows at the top and bottom of stairs above ground floor level, in direct line with the direction of travel, that face east or west should be avoided due to the increased risk of glare from the rising or setting sun.

Artificial lighting should provide an average of 200 lux on the stair treads throughout the stairwell and a minimum 100 lux at all surfaces around the staircase.

Lighting should ensure that the stairs are easily identifiable when approaching from either direction.

The lighting solution should ensure differentiation between treads and risers.

All lighting should be diffused to prevent glare when approaching or using the stairs.

Switching of artificial lighting on the stairs should be available at both the top and the bottom of the staircase.

Any lamps that are supplied should provide the adequate lux levels instantly, ie instant full illumination.

Consideration should be given to providing reasonable accessibility for changing light bulbs. Fluorescent long-life lamps can reduce the need for lamp changing. Also, fittings that incorporate more than one lamp have the advantage of providing some light after one lamp has blown. However, the need for instant illumination to the required lux levels should not be compromised.

### 6.3.8 General storage

All doors to storage cupboards, service cupboards, etc. should ideally be sliding or at least should not protrude into the circulation space.

All storage cupboards should have switched interior electric lights as detailed below.

Walk-in cupboards should be lit internally with bulkhead luminaires, completely diffused to avoid glare.

Other cupboards should be lit with lighting similar to under-unit lighting in kitchens (see section 8.3.8) ensuring that sufficient shielding or diffusing is provided to avoid glare.

Switches to all cupboard lights should turn the light(s) off automatically after a short period of time. Care should be taken to locate the switch in an accessible position while reducing the risk of it accidentally being switched on by items falling against it. The switch should contrast against the background.

All ironmongery on storage cupboards should contrast with its background and be shaped to prevent clothing from snagging.

### 6.3.9 General lighting

The general lighting solution installed, excluding task and portable lighting, should provide an average illuminance level on the floor of 200 lux. The highest levels of illuminance should be achieved on the surfaces at the top and bottom of the staircase to assist in stepping on and off the stair.

All ceiling-mounted luminaires and wall-mounted luminaires should be adequately shaded/diffused to prevent glare.

### 6.3.10 Task lighting

Additional task lighting either fitted or enabled via electrical sockets for portable lights should be available at the location of the telephone socket (where relevant) and at the front door to assist in finding keys and in locating the door handle and the lock.

# CHAPTER 7
# LIVING AREAS

**7.1 PRINCIPLE**

- **Ensure that space is available for the usual range of furniture with clear space to circulate and features to maximise functional vision.**

**7.2 DESIGN CONSIDERATIONS**

Consider the shape of the room(s) as well as the floor area. Square and rectangular rooms will assist in practical furniture layouts with squarer rooms being the most practical.

Additional space may be required to accommodate low vision or assistive equipment without creating a hazardous or cluttered room. The room should be able to accommodate a limited amount of additional equipment without it dominating the room and thereby drawing attention to the occupier's sight loss.

People with sight loss may require a furniture layout that enables the centre of the room to be clear of all items. Adequate clear wall space will therefore be required to accommodate all the typical furniture items.

In addition to living space and typical living room furniture, a dining space should be identified, sufficient for a permanently positioned dining table and chairs related to the designed occupancy level.

Studies by the University of Reading's Research Group for Inclusive Environments have shown that typical living rooms, when using artificial lighting tend to be one of the least well-lit rooms in the home. In addition, traditional overhead ceiling lights have a high incidence of glare due to inadequate shielding of the lamp. General lighting provision should overcome these tendencies.

Consideration should be given to all the probable locations for reading, writing and eating within living spaces and to ensure that optimum task lighting is achievable in these locations. Where task locations are known, fixed task lighting may be appropriate. In other locations or possible task locations, designers should ensure an adequate

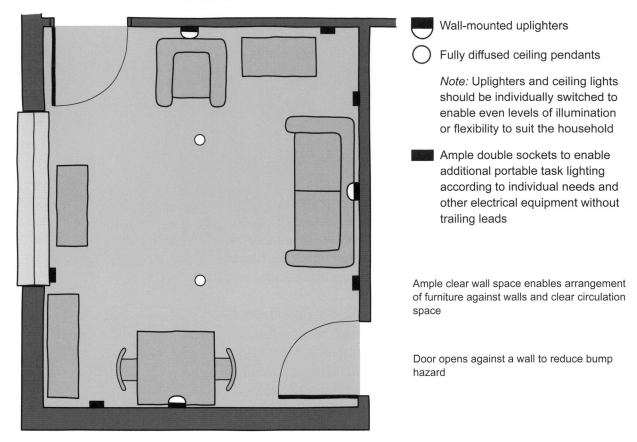

Wall-mounted uplighters

Fully diffused ceiling pendants

*Note:* Uplighters and ceiling lights should be individually switched to enable even levels of illumination or flexibility to suit the household

Ample double sockets to enable additional portable task lighting according to individual needs and other electrical equipment without trailing leads

Ample clear wall space enables arrangement of furniture against walls and clear circulation space

Door opens against a wall to reduce bump hazard

*Figure 8:* Typical living room features

provision of electrical sockets to enable the use of portable task lighting without the need for trailing leads.

In dwellings on two or more storeys the living room should be located below a main bedroom so that a through-floor lift could be installed in the future from the living room to the bedroom if required.

## 7.3 REQUIREMENTS

### 7.3.1 Space standards

Layout planning should avoid the creation of excessively long and narrow rooms.

The size and shape of the room, position of windows, doors, fixtures and fittings should enable a furniture layout that is suitable for the designed occupancy and permit arrangement of the furniture against the walls, leaving the centre of the room and logical circulation routes free of all obstructions. Squarer rooms are more likely to enable this. An identified area for a permanent dining table and chairs relevant to the occupancy level should be included (Figure 8).

Unhindered access to heating, window controls/handles and electrical controls should also be possible given the above furniture layout.

Dwellings over two or more storeys should have a living room located under a main bedroom, the bedroom being adjacent to the bathroom, with an identified lift space. The floor joists over the lift space should be trimmed to provide a knock-out panel, clear of all services, for a through-floor domestic wheelchair user's lift if needed in the future.

## 7.3.2 General lighting

An even level of light should be provided by the general lighting provision. Dark corners should be avoided. Luminaires should be positioned to minimise shadows caused by objects and individuals when performing tasks within the room (Figure 8).

A minimum of two ceiling luminaires should be provided. It is essential that these be provided with adequate shielding/shading that eliminates glare from all areas of the room (Figure 8).

Additional wall uplighters that contain shades/diffusers to prevent glare from below should also be provided (Figure 8).

The ceiling lights and wall uplighters should be individually switched.

The general lighting solution installed, excluding task and portable lighting, should enable a minimum illuminance of 150 lux on the floor surface.

## 7.3.3 Task lighting

Where task areas are identified (eg a defined dining area) fixed task lighting which may take the form of additional uplighters or other fully diffusing luminaires should be provided (Figures 8 and 9).

Each fixed task light should be individually switched to maximise flexibility of lighting within the room, and together with the general lighting should be capable of

*Figure 9:* **(a)** Inadequate and uneven lighting, **(b)** good lighting options

achieving the following minimum level of illuminance onto the task surfaces:

- reading and writing    400 lux,

- having a meal          300 lux.

Wherever possible, dimming should be available.

The designer should ensure that there is an ample supply of electrical sockets to enable portable task lighting in all other probable task areas without the need for trailing leads across any circulation route.

## Profile 2: Using tactile clues to organise the living space

**Alice, a young woman with optic atrophy, has so little functional vision that for her, tactile information about her surroundings is more important than visual information.**

*'I have a system for setting up my living space.'*

In the two-bedroom flat she shares with her partner and another flatmate, Alice has set up her living space (often using tactile stickers) and arranged her possessions how she needs them. Her vision is 'light perception' only; she sees in 'shades' of darkness or lightness with no perception of shape or colour, but can locate doors and windows. Her vision is constant and she uses her light perception to avoid obstacles. However, if Alice changes her light perception (eg by wearing a hat with a brim that shades her eyes) she will bump into things.

Alice's 'system' for organising her living space means that she can cope in any kind of accommodation, but she finds the current flat, which was built for people with sight loss, more user-friendly. Her partner, who also has sight loss, has different design and adaptation needs, but the flat also provides for these without conflicting with Alice's needs.

Alice previously lived in less spacious accommodation and she and her partner appreciate the extra space. Alice no longer has to rely on a laptop as there is now room for a desktop computer with screen-reading technology. The additional space also helps them avoid placing things where they may become obstacles. The flat is about to be fitted with blinds so that the levels of daylight are more controllable to help Alice's partner.

Other assistive equipment in the flat includes:

- 'talking' bathroom scales,
- digital radio, and
- a 'talking' microwave.

*'I have a colour detector which helps me decide what to wear and sort clothes for washing.'*

A domestic support worker is available but the flatmates rarely use this service. They do have a cleaner, but this is more for convenience than a necessity as they are able to share the responsibility for cleaning. A volunteer comes every 2-3 weeks to assist with personal affairs, such as reading letters and forms, which maintains Alice's sense of independence.

Alice has a job and, despite reservations about travelling on public transport at night, she generally gets to everywhere she wants to go. She does not have a guide dog but occasionally uses a cane outside the home. Transport links are good, and there are useful facilities and shops nearby.

# CHAPTER 8
# KITCHENS

**8.1 PRINCIPLE**

- **Maximise functional vision and minimise obstacles and hazards within a functional kitchen.**

**8.2 DESIGN CONSIDERATIONS**

A logical and convenient working layout that enables unobstructed movement between functional equipment and surfaces is essential.

The fridge/food storage, sink, hob, oven and ample functional work surfaces should be positioned to enable easy movement between each and a logical food preparation, cooking and serving sequence. This is a major safety consideration as well as a practical issue. The sink and hob should be close together to assist safe transfer of hot pans, etc.

Designers should note that kitchen users with sight loss may wish to keep more portable appliances on the work surface so ample work surfaces should be specified.

Kitchens have many horizontal and vertical surfaces, and more controls and items of equipment than any other room in the dwelling. Tonal and colour contrasts between adjacent surfaces, equipment and their background, controls and background to the controls are essential.

Kitchens also have a high incidence of finishes that may be a potential source of glare. Shiny surfaces, typical on kitchen appliances and equipment, some kitchen worktops and unit doors/drawers, and some splash-backs may be a problem for people with sight loss. Specifiers should seek to minimise glossy, mirror-like or shiny finishes on all surfaces. Similarly, although more difficult with appliances and equipment, specified items should reduce reflective and shiny finishes as far as possible (eg brushed satin instead of shiny chrome or stainless steel). Highly glossy ceramic hobs should not be specified.

The locating of, and clues to assist in the use of, controls on any specified appliances should be considered. Controls prominent in contrast and physical form will assist some users. However, this should be achieved while avoiding the appearance of 'special equipment'. Controls that are tactile, especially in determining the 'off' and other defined settings, or that move through settings with defined 'clicks' or defined 'movement resistance' will also assist users. Controls should also be suitable for a wide range of people and age groups, including those with limited hand dexterity.

The concentration of cupboard doors in a kitchen creates potential for numerous bump hazards when they are left open or ajar. Units with sliding doors will overcome this potential hazard but have the disadvantages of restricted access, troublesome operation unless of the highest quality, and limited market choice. Consideration of the long-term viability for replacement components for maintenance on 'untypical' kitchen units also needs to be considered. Hinges that allow doors to swing lightly to a full 180° from the shut position if knocked can reduce the risk of accidents caused by bumping into doors left open or ajar. Incorporating areas of functional open shelving at suitable locations can also assist in kitchen use while reducing the potential problem of bumping into doors that have been left ajar.

Incorporating dedicated task lighting in addition to the general lighting may assist or enable individuals to perform the numerous kitchen activities. Areas of frequent task activity should be located adjacent to windows. (See *Chapter 11* for issues regarding the control of potential glare from windows.)

## 8.3 REQUIREMENTS

### 8.3.1 Layout

An efficient layout enabling an effective working relationship between the fridge, sink, hob and oven is essential.

Whenever possible, sinks and drainers should be located in front of a window to offer potential for maximising natural light in this task area.

There should be an unbroken work surface between the sink/drainer and the hob which should be close together, ie:

- a minimum distance apart of 400 mm, and

- a maximum distance apart of 1200 mm.

Unbroken work surfaces are required in any other location that may require the movement of pots, pans and bowls from one task area to another.

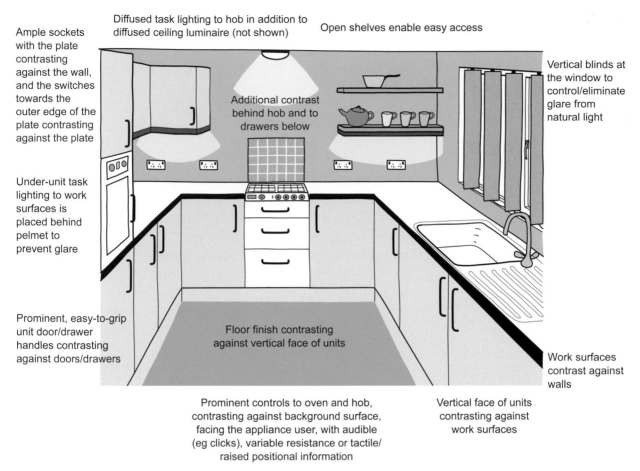

Ample sockets with the plate contrasting against the wall, and the switches towards the outer edge of the plate contrasting against the plate

Diffused task lighting to hob in addition to diffused ceiling luminaire (not shown)

Open shelves enable easy access

Vertical blinds at the window to control/eliminate glare from natural light

Additional contrast behind hob and to drawers below

Under-unit task lighting to work surfaces is placed behind pelmet to prevent glare

Prominent, easy-to-grip unit door/drawer handles contrasting against doors/drawers

Floor finish contrasting against vertical face of units

Work surfaces contrast against walls

Prominent controls to oven and hob, contrasting against background surface, facing the appliance user, with audible (eg clicks), variable resistance or tactile/ raised positional information

Vertical face of units contrasting against work surfaces

*Figure 10:* Typical kitchen details

There should be a clear work surface of at least 400 mm to both sides of the hob surface.

Clear work surfaces of at least 600 mm should be adjacent to the cooker and fridge spaces.

There should be at least two work surfaces, one of which should be a minimum 1200 mm wide.

The end of worktop runs should, whenever possible, abut a side wall or tall cupboard to prevent objects falling off or being knocked off the open end of the worktop.

Electrical sockets (see section 13.3.2) should be ample and well dispersed to enable portable appliances to be sensibly located and dispersed to avoid unnecessary clusters which may be confusing and also clutter up work surfaces.

There should be a clear 1200 mm in front of all appliances, base units and tall units.

## 8.3.2 Units and worktops

Worktops and work surfaces should be non-reflective and 'plain' (ie not prominently patterned). They should have a minimum 30 mm thickness with a post formed rounded front edge. Worktop ends should be factory cut and sealed with matching laminate.

Mastic sealant should be applied at the back end of all worktops and at ends that abut a wall or tall unit.

Units should either have sliding doors on quality running mechanisms, or where this is not practical due to market supply or ongoing maintenance concerns, robust hinges that will operate through 180° so that a door left open or ajar will swing freely out of the way flush to adjacent cupboards should someone bump into it. Any hinged door should have an edge that contrasts with the front and back surface finish.

Unit door, drawer and carcase finishes should be plain and reasonably matt (ie non-glossy).

All storage within units should be readily accessible. High-level storage, not reachable from a standing position, should be avoided unless pull-down storage compartments accessible from a standing position are incorporated. Corner units should be supplied with carousel baskets.

Wall cupboards are not to be located over the sink, draining board or hob/cooker.

All handles on doors and drawers should be easy to locate, in a consistent position on all doors, be suitable for people with limited hand dexterity and not likely to cause clothing to snag on them. See section 8.3.3 below for contrasting requirements and finish.

The minimum storage space (base + wall units) required is:

1–2 person households        $1.5 \ m^3$

3–4 person households        $2.1 \ m^3$

5–5+ person households       $2.2 \ m^3$

*plus:*

a tall broom cupboard unless a separate built-in broom/ cleaning appliance cupboard is located elsewhere.

### 8.3.3 Colour and tonal contrasts

The work surface should contrast against the colour of the matt wall tiling.

The door and drawer fronts should contrast against the work surface and the floor finish.

The door/drawer handles/ironmongery should contrast with the door/drawer and should not have a glossy (mirror-like) finish.

The plinth at the foot of base units should match the door colour of the units, should not be specularly reflective, and should contrast with the floor finish.

### 8.3.4 Appliances and appliance spaces

The designer should provide a clear serviced 600 × 600 mm fridge/freezer space in all kitchens.

A built-in oven and hob within a dedicated 600 × 600 mm appliance space should be provided in all kitchens connected to the relevant services. The type of oven and hob should be agreed with the client. Service connections for both gas (where available) and electricity should be provided regardless of the type of oven and hob initially supplied.

A 650 mm wide × 600 mm deep clear washing machine space with hot and cold water and drainage connections should be provided in all kitchens or utility rooms unless communal laundry facilities are provided.

The designer should identify work surface space for additional free-standing appliances (eg microwave), with associated electrical sockets, that does not interfere with food preparation surfaces.

In dwellings designed for occupancy of 5 or more people, a further 600 × 600 mm appliance space should be provided with both hot and cold water services and an electrical socket.

The provision of any kitchen appliances within the required appliance spaces should be discussed with the client.

All appliances supplied should have both clear and distinct controls and indicators and have the ability to provide tactile controls/information (ie involve 'clicks' when moving the control to a pre-determined position) or move with variable resistance to pre-determined settings, or provide audible or tactile/raised positional information.

All controls and indicators on any appliance supplied should be positioned at the front of the appliance to enable the user to front the control/indicator directly. Side or rear controls and indicators should be avoided.

Controls on appliances should contrast against their background and should not be backed by glass or a mirror-like surface.

Appliances themselves should not have highly glossy surfaces (eg they should have a satin or brushed finish, rather than polished stainless steel or chrome). Ceramic hobs are often highly reflective/mirror-like and may be problematic.

**8.3.5 Sinks**   Sink and drainer surfaces should not be mirror-like or shiny.

**8.3.6 Taps**   Hot and cold taps should be positioned consistently throughout each dwelling and any communal facilities.

The form of taps and use of mixers should also be consistent throughout each dwelling and communal facilities.

Taps with short levers are preferred. Any alternative should be approved by the client in advance.

Hot and cold labelling should be readily apparent and enable distinction by touch. Large, red and blue 'H' and 'C' indicators, contrasting with their background, and raised to enable distinction by touch would be ideal.

**8.3.7 General lighting**   Ceiling-mounted fluorescent luminaires are required. These should be high-frequency type, fitted with diffusers, enabling a minimum average level of 200 lux on the floor surface, and connected to an individual switch.

**8.3.8 Task lighting**   High-frequency, non-flicker, fluorescent luminaires should be installed under wall units to give an even illumination to the entire work surface below. These should be carefully positioned and adequately shielded to prevent glare for all potential kitchen users. The task and general lighting should enable a 500 lux level on the work surface (Figure 11).

Additional task lighting, or additional high-frequency fluorescent luminaires, individually switched, should be provided for any of the following tasks areas not catered for by the under-wall-unit lighting or general lighting, to achieve the following lux levels:

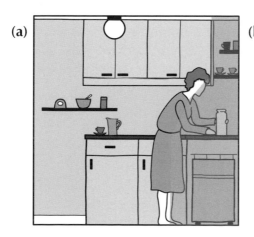

*Figure 11:* **(a)** No task lighting, **(b)** good task lighting

- cooking                          500 lux,

- washing up                    300 lux,

- other work surfaces    500 lux.

All task lighting should avoid shadows being cast over the task space by the task performer.

# CHAPTER 9
# BATHROOMS AND WCs

## 9.1 PRINCIPLE

- **Enable independence by providing easy access to and within the bathroom and maximise functional vision for use of the facilities.**

## 9.2 DESIGN CONSIDERATIONS

The provision of bathroom and toilet facilities should suit the size of household.

Fully accessible toilet facilities and drainage for an accessible shower should be provided on the entrance level to every dwelling.

The designer should consider how to provide the simplest relationship and travel route between bedrooms and bathrooms. Occupancy levels and the range of bathroom facilities should inform possibilities for en-suite arrangements or for providing a direct link between a bathroom and a bedroom. The minimum provision should be a bathroom immediately adjacent to a main bedroom with the possibility for a connecting door (via a knock-out panel) between the two rooms.

Bathroom fixtures and fittings, by their nature, need to be located by the bathroom user as easily as possible, and can also be obstacle hazards for people not familiar with the bathroom layout. Logical layouts, providing relevant colour contrasts, suitable finishes and optimum lighting can all assist in the easy and safe use of the bathroom.

Sanitary fittings and many bathroom fixtures and controls tend to have a shiny finish which can become a source of glare. Specifiers should seek to reduce the amount of mirror-like reflective surfaces and finishes as far as is possible.

## 9.3 REQUIREMENTS

### 9.3.1 General

The minimum requirement on the entrance level of all dwellings (regardless of dwelling form) is a fully wheelchair-accessible WC with drainage in the floor to enable an accessible shower to be provided if required. These provisions may be incorporated into the bathroom of a flat or bungalow.

The minimum provision for all dwellings is an effective and logical bathroom layout with sufficient space for a fully accessible showering area, and a toilet and wash hand basin, both with ease of access for people with impaired mobility. This should have an access door off the hallway/ landing.

In addition to the minimum provision above, a bath should be provided in all dwellings designed for occupancy of 4 or more persons, and/or in dwellings with two bathrooms.

A bathroom should be located adjacent to a main bedroom in every dwelling. En-suite arrangements should suit the household occupancy and the range of facilities provided, but the minimum provision for this is the provision of a knock-out panel between the two rooms to enable easy installation of a connecting door if required. Bathroom and bedroom layouts and drainage/service runs should enable this installation without requiring alteration.

## 9.3.2 WCs

Every dwelling should have a fully wheelchair-accessible WC on the entrance level. In single-storey flats and bungalows this could be in the main bathroom. A fully wheelchair-accessible WC requires the centre line of the WC to be located between 400 mm and 500 mm (450 mm optimum) off a side wall, and a clear 1000 mm from the centre line to the other side for the entire depth of the toilet bowl and cistern (or equivalent depth if a concealed cistern). A clear 1100 mm is also required to the front of the toilet bowl.

All other WCs, where provided within dwellings (in addition to the fully accessible provision above), should have 'ease of access'. This requires a clear 1000 mm from the centre line to one side of the toilet bowl for the full depth of the toilet bowl (but not necessarily the cistern).

All WCs should be either close-coupled or incorporate a concealed cistern. Any concealed cistern should have easy and adequate access for maintenance of cistern components.

Flush handles on close-coupled cisterns should be the large spatula type, located away from the corner of the room. Similar provision, or a large flush push button, is required on concealed cisterns. In the latter case, the large push button should also be easily located by feel from the surrounding surface. Both types of flush control should contrast against their background/surrounding surface.

All WC seats and covers should contrast against the WC bowl, the cistern/background and the floor.

### 9.3.3 Showers

Drainage provision and capped-off electrical and water services for an accessible shower (see below) should be provided as the minimum provision on the entrance level of every dwelling. This could be automatically provided within the shower provision in the main bathroom of single-storey flats and bungalows.

An accessible shower should be provided in every single-storey dwelling (ie all flats and bungalows). A flush floor drainage gulley or a level grating over a recessed shower tray is the preferred provision: any proposed alternative provision (eg a proprietary accessible shower tray and enclosure) *must* be approved by the client at the initial design stage.

All shower gulleys/level gratings should be set into a non-slip floor finish. Where possible, gulleys should be located close to a corner of a room so that water will drain away from the centre of the room. Where level gratings over recessed shower trays are specified, the gratings should be easy to lift/lower, and be lightweight to enable cleaning of the tray below.

Slight falls in the non-slip floor, sufficient to enable drainage to the floor gulley or grating are required. Gradients should be the minimum required to effect full drainage but should not exceed 1:50.

There should not be any thresholds or water bars at the doorway to the bathroom.

The minimum showering activity area should be 1000 mm × 1000 mm.

A fold-down seat should be provided within the showering area. This should contrast against the wall on which it is fitted. The height of the seat should preferably be set to suit the user (where this is known). Where this is not known, the seat surface should be set at 480 mm from the floor.

Showering areas should be adequately curtained or screened to assist in containing water. Shower curtains, where provided, should contrast in colour and tone with adjacent surfaces/general background. Shower screens, where provided, should have neither a clear nor a mirror-like reflective finish. They should also contrast with adjacent surfaces and the general background. Any protruding edge of a shower screen should contrast distinctly to minimise the risk of a person walking into it.

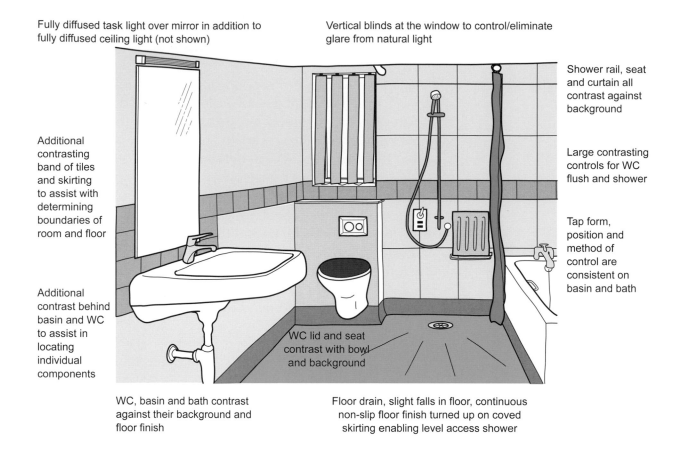

Fully diffused task light over mirror in addition to fully diffused ceiling light (not shown)

Vertical blinds at the window to control/eliminate glare from natural light

Shower rail, seat and curtain all contrast against background

Additional contrasting band of tiles and skirting to assist with determining boundaries of room and floor

Large contrasting controls for WC flush and shower

Additional contrast behind basin and WC to assist in locating individual components

Tap form, position and method of control are consistent on basin and bath

WC lid and seat contrast with bowl and background

WC, basin and bath contrast against their background and floor finish

Floor drain, slight falls in floor, continuous non-slip floor finish turned up on coved skirting enabling level access shower

*Figure 12:* Typical bathroom details

Any leading edge of a shower screen door should also contrast against the door/screen itself. Shower curtains, if possible, should also have a contrasted trim along the leading edge to assist in locating its pull edge. Note that any screen/door should not contain any threshold/raised profile that would interfere with the level/accessible entry to the showering area.

The shower controls should be large and tactile, and contrast with their background. Large push button controls are required for the principal on/off operations. Light indicators of different colours should show when the shower is on standby mode and when it is on. A safety temperature lock, which prevents the user from accidentally selecting an excessively hot or scalding temperature, should be incorporated.

The shower head should be easily reachable, and easily adjusted in both height and direction. It, and any associated rail, should not have a highly glossy finish. They should contrast against their background.

The shower unit should not have a highly reflective finish and should contrast against its background.

### 9.3.4 Baths

In addition to the shower provision described above, baths should be provided in all dwellings with a designed occupancy level of 4 or more persons.

All baths should be steel, 1700 mm in length, approximately 700–750 mm wide, of regular/standard shape, and have slip-resistant flat bottoms and recessed hand grips on both sides.

Bath plugs should be the plunger type or a similar simple mechanism incorporated within the waste outlet.

### 9.3.5 Basins

Basins should be curved and not contain sharp corners.

Basin plugs should be the plunger type or a similar simple mechanism incorporated within the waste outlet.

### 9.3.6 Taps

All taps should be consistent in their position, general form, and operating lever to those in the kitchen. Lever taps with short levers are the preferred option.

Hot and cold taps should be identifiable by touch as well as having bold visual clues. Large raised tactile 'H' and 'C' lettering, coloured red and blue, contrasting against the background, would be ideal.

Water supplies to hot taps should be linked to a thermostatic control that will prevent the water reaching scalding temperature.

### 9.3.7 Wall finish

Walls in all bath/shower rooms and WCs should be fully tiled in plain matt or satin finish tiles.

Increased contrast banding of tiles above the coved skirting and above baths and basins will assist in determining the boundaries of the room and the location of sanitary fittings.

### 9.3.8 Floor finish

A coved skirting is required around the perimeter of all bath/shower rooms and WCs. This should also run along the base of any bath provided.

A non-slip, non-reflective, plain (not prominently patterned), vinyl sheet flooring, with welded joints turned up at the integral coved skirting is required. The floor finish should be capable of complete water tightness to take water from the shower to the integral gulley.

### 9.3.9 Contrasts

Floor finishes should contrast against wall finishes.

Wall finishes should contrast against the floor and ceiling finish.

Sanitary ware should contrast against both the floor finish and the adjacent wall/other finishes.

Tile banding/blocking may be assistive in increasing contrasts between the wall and floor, behind sanitary ware, and also in defining the showering area. However, banding and blocking should be limited, and should not detract from an overall domestic and stylish appearance.

Taps should contrast against their background.

Hot and cold tactile lettering on taps (or equivalent tactile information to determine hot and cold taps) should contrast against the tap.

Shower units, shower heads and slider rails should contrast against their background.

Shower screens/curtains should contrast against the floor and their general background. Any protruding or leading edge should have a further contrasting band contrasting against the overall screen/door/curtain.

## 9.3.10 Adaptability/grab rails

Wall construction should be sufficiently robust for the firm fixing of grab rails at any location. Ply sheet cladding may be a suitable option for some forms of construction such as lightweight stud partitions.

Grab rails should not generally be fitted as their need and location is likely to be specific to the individual occupier. If the need for any grab rail is known and specified, the rail(s) should contrast against the wall on which they are fitted, be non-glossy (matt finish) and have a good integral grip.

Modern methods of construction (eg bathroom pods) should ensure that the form of construction and offsite manufacturing enable simple fixing for the above grab rail requirement (at any location) and provide for any required knock-out panel as detailed below.

The provision of a knock-out panel for a possible future door between the bathroom and a main bedroom, free of all services, is required if no direct access is already available.

## 9.3.11 General lighting

The general lighting and task lighting (excluding the mirror light) should provide an even illumination over the entire floor area averaging 200 lux.

The lighting should be connected to a switch outside the bathroom door.

All bathroom luminaires should meet the IP rating required for their location in accordance with safety zoning.

## 9.3.12 Task lighting

Mirror lights, either over mirrors or to both sides of the mirror over basins, should be provided. They should be fully enclosed within diffusers and set on the wall to minimise the risk of glare from light reflecting in the mirror. Any pull-cord to the mirror lights should contrast against its background. This task lighting, together with any general lighting, should be able to produce a level of 200 lux on the task area and basin rim.

Other task lighting for showering/bathing is also required. However, this may be incorporated within the general lighting provision as long as no shadows from the user or other fixed objects are cast over controls within the task area. A 200 lux level is required on the controls (shower controls and bath taps) and key surfaces (shower floor and seat, bath bottom and rim) in these task areas.

All task luminaires should meet the IP rating required for their location in accordance with safety zoning.

# CHAPTER 10
# BEDROOMS

## 10.1 PRINCIPLE

- **Ensure sufficient space for the usual range of furniture and clear routes to enter, approach all furniture, windows and controls with general and specific task lighting to assist in dressing and personal grooming.**

## 10.2 DESIGN CONSIDERATIONS

Bedrooms should be located close to the bathroom(s) with simple unobstructed routes between the rooms.

Depending on occupancy levels and the number of bathrooms, consider whether providing a connecting door between a main bedroom and a bathroom is desirable.

In two-storey housing a main bedroom should be over a living room in order to facilitate a through-floor wheelchair users lift from the living room below (see section 7.3.1). It is preferable for this main bedroom to have the most direct access route to a bathroom.

One-bedroom dwellings should generally be avoided. This will assist in normalising social relationships where necessary, particularly for those more vulnerable or less able to socialise externally.

## 10.3 REQUIREMENTS

### 10.3.1 General

A double bedroom should be provided in every dwelling. It is desirable that a second bedroom should also be provided unless there is guest accommodation available within communal facilities.

A main bedroom should be immediately adjacent to a bathroom with potential for a connecting door between the two rooms.

In two-storey housing a main bedroom should be over a living room to facilitate a through-floor wheelchair user's lift from the living room below (see section 7.3.1). A knock-out panel in the floor construction should be provided to facilitate this possible future adaptation.

### 10.3.2 Space standards

Rooms should be able to accommodate the usual full range of furniture and provide clear access routes to each item (including both sides of a double bed), the window and all controls. Main bedrooms adjacent to bathrooms should also provide a clear route to any potential connecting door.

### 10.3.3 Storage

All doors to built-in wardrobes should either be sliding or they should not protrude into the circulation space.

All built-in wardrobes should have switched interior electric lights. The switch should contrast against its background and turn the light off automatically after a short period of time. The switch should be located in an accessible position that also reduces the risk of it being accidentally switched on by items falling against it.

The lighting within wardrobes should be high-frequency (no flicker) fluorescent type, fitted with diffusers and positioned to maximise light on clothing within the cupboards while avoiding glare to the user.

### 10.3.4 General lighting

The general lighting provision, excluding task and portable lighting, should provide a minimum illuminance of 150 lux on the floor.

Ceiling lights should be fully shaded from below to prevent glare from the lamp from any position in the room.

The use of wall-mounted uplighting shaded from below (eg positioned over the head of the bed) is also recommended.

Each light should be individually switched.

### 10.3.5 Task lighting

Where not provided by general lighting, additional task lighting and/or provision of ample electrical sockets should enable the following illuminance levels when performing the following tasks.

Choosing clothes:

- from drawers: 150 lux horizontally on the open drawer,

- from wardrobes: 150 lux vertically on the hanging clothes

Personal grooming at dressing table:

- 200 lux on the dressing table surface

Putting on shoes:

- 150 lux on the floor

Reading in bed:

- 400 lux on the pillow

Ensure task lighting is not shielded by a person when performing the task.

Each task light should be individually switched and have sufficient diffusers to prevent glare.

# SECTION 3
## General services and components

# CHAPTER 11
# WINDOWS

## 11.1 PRINCIPLE

- **Maximise natural light while ensuring shading is achievable.**

## 11.2 DESIGN CONSIDERATIONS

While achieving the principle of maximising natural light, designers should also consider the needs of people who will need to control or reduce the amount of natural light. The form of windows and their controls specified should therefore enable the fixing of vertical Venetian blinds within the window recess.

Window controls should cater for a variety of needs: they should be accessible and easy to operate, and offer ventilation while maintaining a high level of security.

Natural light within a room should be as evenly distributed as possible. Where possible, consider providing a second window to assist this.

Natural light should be maximised in task areas (eg at the kitchen sink, dining table, etc).

Hinged window casements and full-height glazing are potential hazards that may need mitigating.

Although glare can largely be reduced by blinds, in communal areas the differing needs of people may often be in conflict. While no one solution can meet these conflicting needs, designers should be particularly conscious of difficulties that may be caused by glare in critical areas (eg on stairwells) and seek to mitigate the possibility of glare as far as possible (eg by window positioning), while still achieving the required high levels of natural light.

## 11.3 REQUIREMENTS

### 11.3.1 General

Windows should provide a good level of natural light throughout the room. Dark or shady corners or recesses should be avoided.

However, large glazed areas are a potential hazard and a minimum cill height of 600 mm is required wherever possible as the cill will assist in defining the glazed area.

Where full-height glazing is unavoidable (eg a requirement of planning permission), it should have an opaque or near-opaque strip of a minimum width of 150 mm, or series of squares of a minimum of 150 mm square, for the full width of the glazed area. These strips or squares should contrast against their background(s), which may require them to be two-tone. However, they should be unfussy, ie without complicated patterns.

All windows, their opening arrangements and controls should enable the fitting of full-width vertical Venetian and other forms of blind within the window recess. The blinds should be capable of full use and adjustability with the window open or closed and should remain clear of all window controls and the usual curtain fitting/curtain opening/closing arrangements.

In addition to the possible vertical blind fitting, simple curtain fitting should be possible to all windows. Curtains when fitted should operate clear of the operational spaces of the (potential) vertical blinds.

Outward-opening windows at ground-floor level should not be allowed to open over pedestrian routes/paths.

Unless other ventilation strategies are adopted, trickle venting on a fully secure closed window should generally be available as well as a secure night venting option.

### 11.3.2 Positioning

Although maximising natural light on circulation routes and stairs is a priority, windows should not be positioned in locations where they may cause excessive glare and subsequent disorientation.

In individual dwellings, as far as practical, avoid window positions that may cause glare on circulation routes, eg at the end of hallways and the top and bottom of stairs facing the direction of travel, particularly on east- and west-facing walls which may directly catch the rising and setting sun.

In communal areas, such window positions, as indicated above, should be avoided.

### 11.3.3 Ironmongery

Ironmongery should be set at accessible and consistent heights and positions on the windows throughout the property.

The maximum height of window controls/handles is 1200 mm from the floor.

All ironmongery, including restrictors, should be easy to operate.

Locations for automatic window opening controls should be available in logical locations for any window that has limited access for people with restricted mobility (eg behind a kitchen work surface).

### 11.3.4 Security

Window and ironmongery specification should meet *Secured by Design*[5] specification.

All windows should provide a secure night venting option.

### 11.3.5 Finishes

Frames and cills should not have a high gloss finish. A satin finish is required. Factory-applied finishes are preferred.

Ironmongery should not have a highly glossy finish. A matt, satin or brushed finish is required.

### 11.3.6 Contrasts

The colour of the ironmongery should contrast against the frames on which it is fitted.

## Profile 3: Flat for a young couple to meet their conflicting needs

**The challenges of living with sight loss are multiplied if your partner also has sight loss, but of a different type, and his resultant needs are different from your own.**

This is the case with Jane and John, an independent young couple with different eye conditions and different levels of functional vision. They live together in an adapted Victorian flat.

Jane has had cortical blindness since 2002, and has significant sight loss which is constant. She can distinguish lightness and darkness, but not colour.

John had perfect vision until 2001. Diabetic retinopathy, macular degeneration and cataracts in both eyes prevent any vision in his left eye and cause loss of peripheral vision in his right eye. The central vision in the right eye is hazy, with blind and grey spots. Detection of colour or detail is not possible.

When Jane's sight loss forced her to abandon her studies, she managed to secure a studio flat in a supported block designed for people with sight loss. As her current flat is also designed for people with sight loss, it is not necessarily more suitable than her previous property, but the extra space enabled John to move in with her.

Before moving in with Jane, John lived with friends but found the situation difficult. The main challenge was that items were constantly moved around and he didn't know where to find them. His current accommodation is far better suited to his needs, allowing him to be self-sufficient.

Jane and John's flat needed a multiplicity of adaptations to help both of them, including:

- sensor lighting to the rear exit and back garden,
- kitchen task lighting to help John do concentrated tasks such as chopping food, cooking or reading bold print using a magnifying device,
- a handrail up to the front door,
- tactile indicators/surfaces on fixtures and fittings, particularly to help Jane as she prefers low light levels,
- a black chopping board to make it easier to prepare food.

*'Window blinds help adjust the level of light as John has different lighting preferences to me. I need to shut out light to stop headaches.'*

While their home is now well adapted for their current needs, both Jane and John wish it was larger.

*'With a small kitchen it can be difficult to cook as there is limited work surface space and accidents are more likely when the surface space becomes cluttered.'*

More space would also be handy when John's two sons visit.

John and Jane are happy with the location of the property and consider the transport links and local facilities to be good. The area was already familiar to Jane which helped with getting around the locality. The flat is on a main road with bus services but both prefer to use the Tube and they have the option of four Tube lines.

# CHAPTER 12
# HEATING SYSTEMS
# AND GENERAL PLUMBING

**12.1 PRINCIPLE**

- **Provide central heating and plumbing systems that are user-friendly for people with sight loss.**

**12.2 DESIGN CONSIDERATIONS**

Boilers, timers, temperature valves, etc. should all be considered in relation to provision of controls that are accessible, approachable face on, easily identifiable and have clear tactile, coloured clues.

## 12.3 REQUIREMENTS

**12.3.1 Client-related performance requirements**

Systems should include thermostats and other devices/ protective covers, etc. to avoid possible scalding or burns from direct contact with water, pipes or unprotected radiators.

**12.3.2 Boilers**

Boilers should be fully accessible.

They should not protrude over the sink or draining board.

Boiler controls should be easy to use, large and contrast against their background, have tactile indicators and be easily approached enabling face-on viewing.

**12.3.3 General controls**

All controls should be set at consistent heights and at consistent locations as far as is practicable.

Large, embossed tactile controls, with large indicators are required.

**12.3.4 Radiators**

Radiators should not be located close to doors or at prominent positions along circulation routes within the dwelling.

Thermostatic radiator valves (TRVs) should be located at the top of the radiator with indicators as large as possible viewed from above.

**12.3.5 Pipework**

Hot pipes should be concealed or boxed to avoid accidental touch.

**12.3.6 Taps**   Tap positions and form should be consistent throughout the dwelling (see sections 8.3.6 and 9.3.6).

**12.3.7 Stop taps**   Stop taps should be placed in safely and easily accessible locations.

All main stop taps should be labelled. The labels should have raised letters to enable identification of the tap in the need of emergency shut-off.

**12.3.8 Contrasts**   All controls should contrast against their background.

All indicators/gauges within controls should provide contrast against their background.

# CHAPTER 13
# ELECTRICAL (EXCLUDING LIGHTING)

## 13.1 PRINCIPLE

- **Ensure all essential controls are accessible and easy to locate and operate.**

## 13.2 DESIGN CONSIDERATIONS

Consistency of position, height and (where possible) location of similar controls throughout each property and generally throughout the entire development will assist users locating them.

All control fittings should contrast with their background and where possible the actual switch within the fitting should again contrast with the fitting. This consideration should apply to the choice of fixtures and fittings as well as general wall-mounted electrical controls.

As well as providing clues to location, specifiers should also consider audible or tactile clues to the use of all controls (eg the presence of a definite 'click' or resistance movement between defined settings).

The presence or ability to provide audible, tactile or visual clues to firstly, the location of and, secondly, the use of every control needs to be considered throughout specification choices. This applies equally (and is arguably even more helpful) to controls not used regularly (eg circuit breakers).

All controls should be placed at locations considered accessible having regard for probable furniture layouts. In addition, the possible need for controls relating to portable equipment (eg task lighting) and its probable location should be considered and fully catered for.

## 13.3 REQUIREMENTS

### 13.3.1 General

All fixed controls (excluding those on appliances) should be within a range of 450–1200 mm from the floor.

Controls with the same/similar function (eg all light switches) should be positioned consistently and at consistent heights within rooms.

All controls on timers, thermostats, etc., should incorporate large, highly visible markings with tactile indicators, should provide clues to settings via audible 'clicks' or resistance movement between defined settings and should be positioned to enable the user to directly face the control.

## 13.3.2 Sockets

Sockets, as far as practicable given furniture layouts and the need for general accessibility, should be located at consistent distances and locations, a minimum of 300 mm away from doorways and corners.

All sockets should be set at a constant height throughout the dwelling. The height should be between 450 mm (general needs) and 750 mm (wheelchair-user housing) from the floor according to client group (unless over work surfaces).

Double sockets should have the switches to the outer edges of the plate.

All switches within sockets should enable clear tactile recognition of whether the switch is in the 'on' or 'off' position.

Sockets serving appliances located in front of the socket (eg fridges and washing machines) should have accessible isolating switches, with tactile labelling for the relevant appliance.

The designer should ensure that ample sockets are provided (in addition to typical provision) to enable portable task lighting in probable locations as identified in other chapters of this *Guide*. The siting of sockets should be related to furniture layouts and eliminate the need for leads trailing over the floor.

Socket plates should contrast against their background. The switch should also contrast against the socket plate. Socket plates should not have a mirror-like finish (ie not polished metal; satin or brushed metal is acceptable).

The *minimum* number of accessible double sockets per dwelling, excluding those dedicated to appliance spaces, is given in Table 2.

In addition, dedicated appliance sockets should be located within each appliance space, and be linked to remote, tactile labelled isolators as detailed above.

Designers should have regard for all probable portable task lighting requirements and locations in each room when

## Table 2 Minimum number of sockets for each area of the dwelling

| Room/area | Minimum number of double sockets |
|---|---|
| Kitchen:   to serve work surfaces | 3* |
|          general use | 2 |
| Dining area | 2 |
| Living room | 5** |
| Each bedroom | 3 |
| Hallway (ground floor) | 2 |
| Landing | 1 |
| Bathroom | Shaver socket required* |

\*   Exception to the 450 mm height requirement.

\**   Two of these should be positioned adjacent to each other beside (not behind) the probable location of TV/audio equipment.

considering whether the above minimum provision is adequate.

### 13.3.3 Light switching

To maximise flexibility of illuminance levels in and around a room, every general light fitting and individual fixed light to a task area should have individual switching. All switches, regardless of type, should be suitable for people with limited hand dexterity.

Wherever possible, dimmer switches should be provided. However, this should not restrict or conflict with the use of readily obtainable low-energy compact fluorescent lamps that may be required for sustainability or economic considerations.

Where dimmer switches are not installed for particular lamps, it should be possible to easily and cost-effectively retrofit dimmer switches and fit suitable dimmable lamp types for individuals who require increased adjustability in these locations.

Switches should be placed on the opening side of the doorway, at a constant height of 1200 mm throughout the dwelling.

Designers should ensure adequate two-way switching in all hallways, landings and stairwells, and by external doors, to prevent unnecessary travel without light. Switching should be immediately available from the doorway of each bedroom, living room, kitchen and external door.

Bedrooms should have an additional light switch for the general bedroom lighting which is accessible from the bed.

Bathroom lights should be switched to a position immediately adjacent to the opening side of the bathroom door outside the bathroom.

Switch plates should contrast with their background and the switch should contrast with the plate. Switch plates should not have a glossy, mirror-like finish (ie not polished metal; brushed metal or satin stainless steel is acceptable).

### 13.3.4 Telephone points

Telephone points are required in all rooms except bathrooms. These should be located adjacent to electrical sockets to enable portable task lighting to the telephone and possible connection of personal computer/internet/call system/telecare equipment.

### 13.3.5 Television aerial sockets

Television aerial points, adjacent to a socket, are required in all living rooms and bedrooms. These should either be connected to a communal aerial or to an aerial supplied in the loft space or on the roof according to reception.

### 13.3.6 Door entry system/audible caller recognition

Door entry systems or systems to provide audible caller recognition (but manual control of the door lock) may be appropriate. The inclusion and scope of either system should be discussed and determined with the client. Where not provided at the outset, the designer should ensure that future electrical supplies can be easily provided at front doors to enable the simple installation of either without significant disruption or expense.

Where door entry systems are provided, internal control points should be located in the living room and main bedroom (adjacent to the bed). They should be in a matt finish, be fixed/push button types rather than handset-operated, and contrast against their background. The talk/release buttons should also contrast against the unit.

A system enabling audible caller recognition (but maintaining manual door control) may be required instead of a full door entry system. Where provided, the internal control point should be located at a suitable location in the hallway close to the front door. Controls should be in a matt finish, with push button/fixed audible system rather than handsets, and contrast against their background.

### 13.3.7 Extract fans

Unless an alternative ventilation strategy is adopted, bathrooms and WCs should generally be provided with humidistat extract fans operated by the light switch. This will also assist users in knowing if the bathroom light has been left on.

Kitchens should also have humidistat fans or extractors, switched remotely to a wall switch. These fans should have an automatic humidistat control to assist in the control of condensation.

### 13.3.8 Smoke detectors

Hard-wired smoke detectors, in accordance with current building regulations, are required on every floor of every dwelling.

### 13.3.9 Consumer service units

Consumer service units should be located in a readily accessible location. The controls should be provided with tactile information and reachable while standing on the floor. The units should not be positioned at head height unless recessed off any possible circulation route.

### 13.3.10 Capped-off services to enable easy adaptation

The following capped-off services to enable future easy adaptation/installation as required should be provided whenever relevant to the individual dwelling:

- electrical supply for a stair lift,

- electrical supply for a through-lift (from living room to bedroom above),

- electrical supply for a burglar/panic alarm,

- electrical supply for door entry/audible recognition system at front door where not provided at the outset,

- electrical supply for showers where not provided at the outset,

- electrical supply for a light switch in the event that a door may be fitted between bedroom and bathroom.

### 13.3.11 Contrast

All switches and controls should contrast against the plate/background against which they are set.

Switch and socket plates should contrast against their background wall.

# CHAPTER 14
# INTERNAL LIGHTING

**14.1 PRINCIPLES**

- **Achieve optimum levels of general lighting in each room.**
- **Provide or enable optimum levels of task lighting at relevant locations.**
- **Maximise adjustability of all lighting sources.**
- **Eliminate sources of glare**.

**14.2 DESIGN CONSIDERATIONS**

Lighting needs to be considered in accordance with a number of performance criteria and also in relation to key surface finishes. General lighting levels, lighting of surfaces, and specific task lighting all need consideration, and the design of the overall fixed lighting and socket provision (for portable lighting) should ensure that the required and various lighting levels in each room can be achieved.

There are no specific lighting requirements currently published for the domestic environment. However, the Society of Light and Lighting codes[8] do include recommended illuminance levels for tasks and surfaces that can be applied to domestic situations and these are included throughout this *Guide*. However, these recommendations are based on an adult building user between the ages of 40–50 with normal sight. Older people will require more light for the same task regardless of sight loss and greater levels of illuminance may well optimise their visual performance. As a result of ageing of the eye, the 60-year-old needs three times as much light as the 20-year-old to obtain the same amount of light on the retina.

People with sight loss can benefit significantly from obtaining optimum lighting levels for their individual needs. Flexibility and adjustability to suit personal requirements within the overall provision of luminaires and their switching arrangements is therefore essential.

The requirements stated within this *Guide* are based on possible need and the general principle that maximum levels of possible required illuminance should be achievable. However, some people will be seriously adversely affected by light, finding even modest levels of illumination painful, so the ability to adjust the level of each light source (via dimmer switches and/or individual switching of luminaires) should be maximised to provide optimum flexibility. (See *Chapter 13* for more details on light switching). This degree of adjustability will also assist people in achieving maximum functional vision when their eye conditions cause day-to-day differences/preferences in optimum lighting levels.

Providing optimum levels of lighting for each individual at key locations such as stairs and kitchens will significantly reduce the risk of accidents.

Glare from bare lamps can be a particular problem for various eye conditions. Selection of fittings and lamps should have regard for their positioning and the ability to shield users from direct glare from the lamp while in any location in the room.

Lighting equipment and controls should have regard for the need for long-term service, low cost of ownership and use, servicing and ease of re-lamping.

All lighting controls/switching should be simple to use and suitable for people with limited hand dexterity.

Lighting styles selected need to have regard for the domestic setting. The appearance of light fittings, particularly in living areas, is important. Optimum lighting levels should be achieved without fittings appearing untypical of a normal domestic environment.

Different types of lamps available on the market have various characteristics that need to be considered before the selection of fittings. Flicker of some fluorescent lamps can be problematic and should be avoided, and the slow warm-up time to full light output of some low-energy lamps can be potentially dangerous in key locations involving movement (eg the stairs). The ability to shield the room from glare from the lamp completely also needs consideration.

Even levels of light from general lighting will be required, avoiding dark corners and recesses. The position of general lighting needs to have regard for this in conjunction with the need to prevent glare to the room occupants from expected room positions: walking, sitting, lying, etc. The use of less typical (but not uncommon) fittings such as wall lights and uplighters should be considered. These fittings that shield lamps from below can reduce glare and also provide a more even level of illuminance across a room by bouncing light off the walls and ceiling.

Any fixed task light fitting (excluding fluorescent under-cupboard/in-cupboard fittings) should offer flexibility over the position, direction and amount of light to give users the ability to make adjustments to suit their particular requirements.

Flexibility in the control of each light source can also assist an individual who may experience difficulty in adjusting to different lighting levels between different areas or rooms.

Some people may need to get closer to some lamps when performing certain tasks. Task lights containing tungsten or tungsten halogen lamps can become very hot. Task lights with possible close proximity to the user should enable a lower surface temperature lamp (eg a fluorescent tube or compact fluorescent lamp) to be fitted.

Where practical, consider increasing the number of circuit breakers/lighting circuits which may be helpful to the occupant if a circuit trips.

In addition to room lighting, built-in cupboards will also need individually switched lighting within the cupboard, placed to maximise illuminance of objects but fully diffused to prevent glare (see sections 6.3.8 and 10.3.3).

## 14.3 REQUIREMENTS

Ensure an even distribution of light within each room and its major surfaces. A sufficient range of fittings (ceiling-mounted and/or wall-mounted) should be specified to avoid pools of light, shadows and dark corners. The illuminance levels on floor surfaces and other key surfaces as detailed throughout this *Guide* should be achieved.

Designers should enable task lighting to enhance illumination levels at key task areas as stated in the relevant chapters of this *Guide*. Whenever practical and relevant, fittings associated with task lighting should provide flexibility for the position, direction and amount of light needed to suit the individual needs of the user with the ability to reach the maximum illuminance levels as stated (this is not relevant to fluorescent under-unit task lighting in kitchens or cupboard lighting).

Provision of electrical sockets should enable portable task lighting in all identified task or potential task locations where fitted task lights are not provided. Socket provision and location should be adequate to enable this in addition to other typical (non task lighting) socket use and to prevent cables from trailing across the floor.

Fitted task lighting should avoid shadows being cast on the key surface by the task performer.

Designers should ensure that a consistent level of lighting is achievable throughout the dwelling to assist those who experience difficulty in moving between brightly and dimly lit areas and vice versa.

All built-in cupboards should be supplied with compact diffused fluorescent lighting (see sections 6.3.8 and 10.3.3).

Lighting provision throughout each dwelling should be flexible and adjustable so that individuals can tailor it to their particular needs. Each and every general light fitting should therefore be individually switched. Fitted task lighting should also be individually switched. Dimmer switches maximise flexibility and should be provided, wherever possible. However, specifiers should have regard for the potential conflicting user needs with the desire to use easily obtainable low-energy compact fluorescent lamps (which currently are not generally dimmable) in areas of high use.

Glare should be avoided from all possible sources and fully removed from the user's visual field. All types of lamp should be provided with effective shading or diffusers. Any ceiling-mounted fittings should shade the lamp from the side and below when viewed from all positions in the room. Fluorescent tube task lighting under wall cupboards (see kitchens) should have valence pelmets (or equivalent) that ensure the tube is completely shielded from direct viewing by the kitchen user. Other fluorescent lighting should be fully diffused. Shades and diffusers should not cause patterns to be illuminated onto the shade or room surfaces.

Lamps for specified fittings should avoid flicker. Fluorescent lighting should be the high-frequency type with high-frequency control gear to eliminate flicker.

Lamps that require a warm-up time (eg some low-energy lamps) should not be specified for fittings that illuminate circulation routes where instant optimum levels of light are necessary (eg stairs) or rooms that may only be entered for a short period of time.

The colour rendering index of all light sources should achieve at least Ra80. Any lamps provided should meet this performance standard.

Controls and switching should be easy to locate, simple to use, laid out in a logical, uncomplicated manner, and suitable for use by people with limited hand dexterity. *Chapter 13* outlines additional light-switching requirements.

## *Profile 4:* Specific lighting design is essential to enable tasks to be done

**Design features and lighting specification that can maximise what is left of his sight are important to Bob, an independent middle-aged man with variable and deteriorating vision.**

Bob has glaucoma, which causes variation in his vision, and a condition similar to macular degeneration which causes partial sight loss. Bob was required to surrender his driver's licence some years ago. His employment was also curtailed due to his sight loss.

Both of Bob's eye conditions are degenerative, which means he will eventually lose his sight completely. Glaucoma is causing a loss of peripheral vision and the macular degeneration is causing a loss of central vision. Because Bob's sight loss is partial at this stage, he finds reading and other concentrated tasks difficult. For example, he can see the beginning and end of a word but has to move his head to see the middle of the word.

Bob lives in a studio flat to which he moved from a much larger house two years ago. His familiarity with his old house, together with better levels of vision, meant that he generally maintained his independence for most of the time at the house. Friends were on hand to assist him when needed. Now, however, Bob lives independently in the flat without needing to call on friends, even though his eyesight has deteriorated.

*'I needed greater control over lighting levels and improved lighting in some places.'*

Bob's current home has been adapted to give better control over general lighting levels and improved lighting at key task locations.

- Diffused fluorescent strip lighting has been installed in some cupboards and under wall units in the kitchen.
- Outside the flat, a fluorescent light has been installed above the keyhole to help in locating the lock.
- 'Yellow' exterior pathway lighting was recently replaced with 'white' lighting which has proved much more helpful.

Further lighting adaptations are soon to be installed that will allow:

- control of distinct lighting levels within the living and separate sleeping area, and
- adjustments so that Bob can watch TV in dim light but also have intense light for reading and task-based activities.

Although the skirting boards are colour-contrasted against light-coloured walls, this feature no longer helps him as his sight has deteriorated. Low items of furniture like the coffee table have been removed as he kept bumping into them.

Cooking can be difficult and Bob has had to buy a dishwasher as he found he was unable to check whether his dishes were clean. He can no longer see the colour graduation indicators on the controls of his cooker and he will require an adaptation, or a cooker with controls providing tactile information, to resolve this difficulty.

A 'talking lift' in the block of flats means that Bob knows when he has arrived at his floor.

Bob has everything he needs nearby, including a supermarket just along the road. Buses are convenient and stop right outside the block. He cannot read LED displays in tube stations and has problems crossing roads due to reduced peripheral vision. While these details limit his independence, they have not deterred him from getting around.

*'I just get on with life.'*

# CHAPTER 15
# SURFACE FINISHES
# AND THEIR CONTRASTS

### 15.1 PRINCIPLE

- **Provide finishes that:**
  - **reduce the potential for glare,**
  - **can assist in differentiating room surfaces and individual objects,**
  - **offer way-finding clues, and**
  - **provide suitable non-slip/non-trip qualities where relevant.**

### 15.2 DESIGN CONSIDERATIONS

Colour contrast, together with good lighting can greatly increase the ability to 'read' the surroundings for people with sight loss, enabling safer navigation around the home and identification of features. See also 'Providing contrast' in *Chapter 2* and *Appendix A*.

Changes in finishes, both tonal and textural, (eg floor colour and texture) can provide clues to identifying one space from another when moving around, or can highlight the approach to features such as steps or front doors.

Colour can also assist as an identifier (eg different colours in the corridors of different floors within a block of flats).

As an overriding consideration, the provision of contrast should not produce a garish or institutional appearance. Tonal contrasts (ie depth of lightness/darkness within a similar colour palette or hue) can achieve the level of contrast required within a subtle overall theme. Contrasts in the depth of a colour will be more effective than a strong contrast of opposing colours of the same depth.

Ceiling, wall, floor, door and opening finishes should all be differentiated from one another with tonal contrasts. However, the resulting appearance should not be anything other than a well designed and decorated typical domestic environment. The provision of tonal colour contrasts should not be immediately apparent or distinctive to sighted people.

Contrasting all controls, indicators, ironmongery, etc. against their backgrounds can assist in their identification and use.

Shiny, highly reflective surfaces can cause glare and should therefore be avoided. Gloss paint, gloss tiling, polished metal are all common finishes that should not be specified for any surface. Similarly, large areas of brilliant white can potentially be a source of glare.

Surfaces should be plain or have small patterns only. Prominent or large-scale patterns should be avoided. This will assist in locating objects on the surface and have less potential to have an overall chaotic appearance.

The use of light colours (which have high reflectance values) for ceilings and walls will increase the amount of inter-reflected light. This will tend to minimise shadows and reduce glare. It is particularly important to have high reflectance values for ceilings and walls when uplighting is used.

## 15.3 REQUIREMENTS

### 15.3.1 General

Reference should be made to the preceding chapters for specific requirements on finishes relating to a component in a particular functional area.

All finishes should be hard-wearing and resistant to damage.

Finishes associated with way-finding by feel (eg handrails) should generally be comfortable and warm to the touch.

### 15.3.2 Wall finishes

All wall finishes should be matt. As a general rule, light colours are required that will assist in the distribution of artificial and natural daylight.

Any wall tiling should be plain and have a matt or satin finish, not a high-gloss finish.

A contrasting border tile should be used around bathrooms and shower rooms/WCs to assist in differentiating the boundaries of the room.

Wall finishes should be differentiated by the use of colour contrast from the ceiling finishes, floor finishes, door finishes and openings.

Tiling in bathrooms, shower rooms and WC compartments should give some colour contrast against adjacent sanitary fittings set against the wall.

Skirting boards should contrast against the wall and floor finishes.

Wall finishes behind kitchen work surfaces should contrast against the work surface.

### 15.3.3 Floor finishes

The designer should ensure any change in finish provides a smooth and flush transition between the finishes which will not wear or fray to become a trip hazard.

Matt finishes are required. Glossy or mirror-like surfaces should not be used on any floor surface or associated trim.

The finish of all floor surfaces should not be highly or distinctly patterned.

All finishes in kitchens, bathrooms and other 'wet' areas should be non-slip.

Carpet with a strong directional weave, pile or nap should be avoided as these can be difficult for people using wheelchairs or mobility aids.

All floor finishes should be easy to clean.

Floor finishes in kitchens should give clear differentiation in contrast against plinth and kitchen unit door and drawer finishes.

All floor finishes should give clear differentiation in colour contrast from skirting and wall finishes.

### 15.3.4 Ceilings

Ceiling finishes should be matt pale tones and offer some contrast against wall finishes.

### 15.3.5 Doors

Doors and their frames should contrast against the surrounding wall, and door furniture should be contrasted against the door.

The leading edge of hinged doors should also contrast against the door colour.

### 15.3.6 Other items

Sockets, switches, handles, etc. should all contrast against their background.

# SECTION 4
## Communal areas

# CHAPTER 16
# COMMUNAL FACILITIES

## 16.1 PRINCIPLES, DESIGN CONSIDERATIONS AND REQUIREMENTS

The principles and design considerations throughout the chapters of this *Guide* relate to specification performance and functional areas for individual dwellings. However, they relate equally to equivalent functional areas and items within communal facilities and are not repeated here. The general principles and considerations throughout the preceding chapters should therefore be applied wherever relevant.

Similarly, the design and specification requirements within each preceding functional chapter should be applied wherever relevant to communal areas unless over-ridden or enhanced by the additional or differing design requirement as listed below.

## 16.2 ADDITIONAL REQUIREMENTS FOR THE EXTERNAL ENVIRONMENT

### 16.2.1 Front garden areas

Small front garden areas should be provided to the front of communal blocks or cluster groups to provide an area of semi-private defensible space, clearly distinguishable from estate/public areas. They should be in keeping and have a consistent appearance with front garden areas elsewhere on the development/neighbouring properties.

Boundary treatments, planting requirements should be in accordance with requirements in *Chapter 4*.

### 16.2.2 Parking

Parking provision for residents and visitors should be discussed with the client and planners. It should be located close to the main entrance.

A barrier and obstacle-free access path in accordance with *Chapter 4* should be maintained from the parking spaces to the main entrance.

### 16.2.3 Approach to the main entrance

Requirements for the approach path are detailed in section 4.3.2.

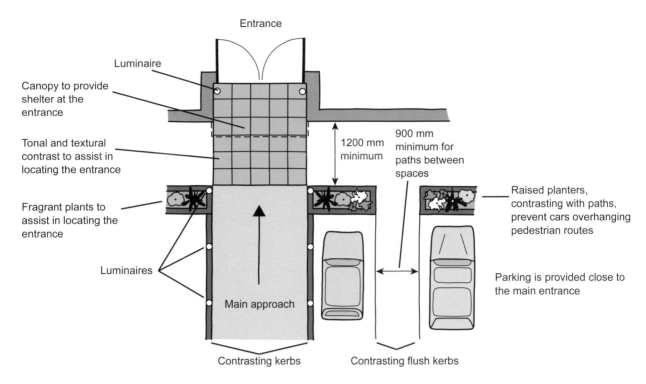

*Figure 13:* Typical external features of a communal entrance

Requirements for lighting to the approach is detailed in section 4.3.7. In addition, designers should consider the need to provide a gradual reduction in illuminance from the inside level to the outside level after dusk, and a further gradual decrease when moving away from the entrance to assist those with adaptation difficulties by providing greater/gradual adaptation times. The opposite applies when entering the building during daylight hours when the decrease in lighting levels from the bright daylight outside should be gradual from the point of entry into the building.

A canopy should be provided within the main entrance design that extends the full width of the door/porch design and has a minimum depth of 1200 mm.

The approach to the door should be 'head on'.

The main entrance should be instantly recognisable. Its design, approach and lighting provision should readily guide visitors unfamiliar with the block towards it. It should have distinctive characteristics that set it apart from other secondary routes and entrances.

## 16.2.4 Entrance

The design considerations and requirements of *Chapter 5* apply with the following additions/upgrades.

The main entrance door(s) should have an effective clear opening width of 1200 mm. This is sufficient to enable an individual with a sighted escort to have clear entry (an individual with a guide dog would require a clear 1100 mm).

Automatic sliding doors (which maximise reduction of potential hazards) are preferred and should be incorporated into new build projects. Automatic hinged doors can potentially be hazardous due to the leading edge being an obstacle when opening towards the user and should only be used in refurbishment when sliding doors are not an option. All leading edges should fold back flush against adjacent walls. The edge of hinged doors should contrast with the face of the door.

Any manual hinged doors should be fitted with an opener that enables the door(s) to be opened with a force not exceeding 20 Newtons. The leading edges should fold back flush against adjacent walls. The edge of hinged doors should contrast with the face of the door.

Revolving doors should not be incorporated.

In addition to requirements in *Chapter 5*, section on *Thresholds and mat wells*, mat wells where provided, should cover the full width of the entrance, be long enough to cover the full turn of a typical wheelchair wheel, and mats should not have a strong directional weave or texture.

A robust door entry system will be required. This should contrast against the wall in which it is set, be logically placed (on the latch side of a single-leaf hinged door), close to the door frame, at a height of 1000–1200 mm from the ground. Buttons/controls should be large, contrast against their background, have large tactile letters/numerals. The system should provide audible feedback on the processes involved with its use.

## 16.2.5 Rear garden area

Whenever the site permits, flatted blocks should provide a small area of communal rear garden accessed off a communal hallway or lounge. This area should be clearly distinct from the private patio areas of ground-floor flats. Planting should be soft (eg without thorns) and aromatic. Gentle water features that involve the sound of water but exclude any depth of water should be considered.

Pathways within and leading to/from the garden should conform to guidance in *Chapter 4*. At least two areas of seating should be provided, this and any other furniture, should be recessed off circulation routes and should conform to guidance in section 3.3.2, avoiding sharp edges or rough textures. Lighting of pathways should conform to guidance in section 4.3.7.

Any raised bed/raised boundary should be a minimum height of 300 mm and logically placed alongside or away from potential pedestrian routes.

Seating areas within the garden and the surrounding layout should maximise the potential for sensory stimulation via aromatic planting and gentle water features.

Orientation and garden layout should aim to enable sunlight to reach seating areas and flower beds for at least part of the year.

### 16.2.6 Waste and refuse disposal

Travel distance for bin collection, bin type and transfer system to the refuse vehicle should be checked with the Local Authority.

Bins should be fully contained in an accessible storage structure, located close to a communal entrance door but away from the main entrance and any window. The structure should not be readily apparent from the main approach to the building.

A separate storage facility adjacent to the bin stores should be provided for household waste that is suitable for recycling.

All stores should be locked with locks suited to enable access by all residents. All ironmongery should be no higher than 1200 mm from the floor and should contrast with its background. The doors themselves should contrast with the store structure and not open over any access route. The edge of hinged doors should contrast with the face of the door.

There should be a short direct path or area of hard landscaping between all external stores and the communal door.

All access paths should conform to guidance in section 4.3.2.

### 16.2.7 External tap

A secure (ie preventing unauthorised use) external tap, should be provided adjacent to the bin stores, and close to the dog run (where provided), metered with the communal water supplies.

### 16.2.8 Guide dog run

Flatted developments with communal external spaces should incorporate an enclosed and gated dog run where guide dogs can be taken for toileting. A smooth concreted floor is required with gradual falls to a foul drain with an easily removable cover. An external tap and hose is required nearby to enable the area to be cleared and washed away via the foul drain. The run should be a minimum size of 2000 mm × 2000 mm; a longer run 2000 mm × 4000 mm is desirable.

## 16.3 ADDITIONAL REQUIREMENTS FOR THE INTERNAL ENVIRONMENT

### 16.3.1 General

The range of communal facilities should be determined by the client. Those facilities described below represent typical facilities but are not an exhaustive list.

Ensure all internal communal areas have a domestic, non-institutional feel/appearance. Their form, scale, finishes and services all need to demonstrate this in their appearance.

All areas should have the appearance of semi-private areas, only open to people with a right to be within the building.

Colour and tonal contrast requirements to finishes and specification items as detailed throughout this *Guide* are again required within a non-garish overall colour scheme. Colour themes should be adopted to assist in determining one area from another (eg lobby from circulation route, different storey levels, etc.)

### 16.3.2 Main entrance lobby

The main entrance lobby immediately inside the main entrance should be provided with a high level of natural light and ventilation. Natural and artificial lighting should enable an illuminance level of 200 lux to be maintained at the entrance area. Artificial lighting enabling the above illuminance level should also incorporate a timed control which could enable the lighting level to be dimmed at required times (eg at night) to a reduced level of 50 lux.

It should be sufficiently large and suitably shaped to enable the area to function as a comfortable sitting area for a number of residents to wait or meet informally without impinging on any circulation routes.

Its spatial and design characteristics, and the lighting should promote a sense of comfort and 'welcome' while also achieving the range of requirements connected with the range of tasks and activities that may occur.

The need for a reception and office facilities should be discussed and determined with the client. Where included, they should be immediately apparent and accessible from the lobby. Their size and form should be determined in discussion with the client according to their management needs and requirements stated below. Ensure access, reception desks, finishes and specification items conform to relevant guidance within this *Guide* and are at heights suitable for all clients, including wheelchair users.

Where offices are provided, ensure sufficient space for necessary workstations and guest seating, including space for a wheelchair user to enter and turn within the room. Lighting provision should enable an illuminance level of 400 lux within the office. A WC compartment to full wheelchair design standards 2200 mm × 1500 mm as shown and detailed in Building Regulation Approved Document M[9] and BS 8300[10] should be located close to the office. Relevant principles and requirements from *Chapter 9* (bathrooms/WCS) should be applied to communal WCs.

Other essential services (eg toilets, main lifts, main staircases, etc.) should all be grouped together and readily accessible from the lobby.

### 16.3.3 Hallways/ corridors

The layout should minimise pedestrian travel distances for residents between their dwelling, the main entrance and communal facilities.

Long corridors/hallways giving a non-domestic or institutional appearance should not be incorporated into the layout.

Dead end hallways should not be incorporated into the layout.

All circulation routes should be short and uncomplicated. Radiators, fire extinguishers and fire doors in the open position should be recessed in alcoves off the line of the circulation route to create a 'smooth' uninterrupted side wall.

A minimum width of 1800 mm is required although this may reduce to 1500 mm for short lengths.

Any turn should preferably be 90°. Oblique angled turns or curves should be avoided whenever possible.

Handrails, circular or with rounded edges, smooth to the touch and uninterrupted by wall support fixings, should be located each side of hallways and as continuous as possible. The end of each section of rail should return to the wall to avoid clothes snagging (see Figure 7).

Steps or ramps should not be incorporated into any hallway.

Windows should not be incorporated into the end of hallways where they would inevitably face the predominant direction of travel.

Natural light should be maximised to reduce dependence on large artificially lit areas.

Natural and artificial lighting should enable an illuminance of 150 lux on the floor.

The overall lighting system should include dimmable luminaires and incorporate timed controls that could enable the average lux level to be reduced to a predetermined level, at predetermined times (eg overnight), in distinct zones/areas if required. Lift lobbies, stairways, corners and junctions should be zoned individually to enable these areas to be dimmed individually according to need, although typically to 50 lux.

Informal seating areas, suitable for residents to stop and chat, should be considered for inclusion into hallway areas. These areas should, however, not interrupt or impinge on simple circulation routes.

Internal hallway doors should be minimised and have a consistent method of opening throughout the building. A single leaf should provide a clear opening width of 825 mm.

Fire doors, where required, should be fitted with automatic devices to enable them to be permanently open under normal circumstances. When open, they should be recessed to be flush with the finished wall surface and hence no barrier to navigation.

## 16.3.4 Doors to communal facilities

Colour contrasts for doors and their adjacent surfaces, door finishes, and door ironmongery, is as required in sections 6.3.3 and 6.3.4.

A clear opening width of 825 mm is required to all doors to communal facilities. A clear space between the keep side of the door and any side wall should be provided and should be at least 300 mm where the door opens towards the user, and at least 200 mm where the door opens away from the user.

Fully glazed doors should not be incorporated. However, glazed vision panels to enable people, including wheelchair users, to see and be seen should be incorporated.

All handles should be lever type and consistently placed on all doors throughout the building.

Door swings should never open out onto a circulation route.

Internal thresholds should not be provided or where a change of finish occurs the transition should be completely flush.

Developments incorporating accommodation for wheelchair users should include a kick plate 300 mm high fixed for the full width to the bottom of the door. Its colour should blend with the door.

WC doors should be provided with a large circular turn vacant/engaged indicator.

### 16.3.5 Stairs

Stair requirements are as detailed in sections 6.3.5–6.3.7, with the following additional requirements.

A minimum clear width of 1200 mm should be maintained.

Risers should be consistent throughout the development within the range 150–170 mm, goings should be consistent throughout the development within the range 250–300 mm.

Distinction/colour contrast between the riser and the stair tread is essential. It should be incorporated in either the finish (or the stair materials where stairs are left with no finish applied), or achieved by the use of lighting where the surface finish of risers and treads is consistent.

Further differentiation of the nosing of each stair tread edge by the use of a contrasting strip is also required.

Stairs should not be located along the normal pedestrian line of travel in a corridor and should involve a conscious 90° turn in direction to begin descent or ascent.

Handrails should be circular mop-stick type, 45–50 mm in diameter, continuous on both sides of the stair at a height of 900 mm above the pitch line of the stair. They should continue for 300 mm beyond the top and bottom of the stairs at a height of 1000 mm above the landing. Handrail ends should be adequately end-stopped or turned in towards the wall. Handrail supports should not interfere with movement or with hands gripping and sliding along the rail.

Handrails that continue along the wall of hallways at the top and bottom of the stairs should have buttons/indicators attached 300 mm from the first and last stair, top and bottom, to indicate the storey level at the start and end of the stairs (1st floor, 2nd floor, etc).

Prominent, contrasting floor numbers with tactile indicators should be located at consistent locations at the top and bottom of every flight.

Balusters or equivalent should prevent a foot or part of a foot protruding off all stairs and associated landings.

It should not be possible for anybody to walk into the edge or underside of any stairway.

Windows in the vicinity of stairs should be fitted with effective blinds to prevent glare. Windows at the top and bottom of flights in line with the direction of travel should be avoided due to the increased risk from glare.

Lighting should generally be in accordance with section 6.3.7, with the exception of switching arrangements and zoning. Each stairway should have its own lighting zone.

16.3.6 Lifts    Lifts should conform to the specification detailed in BS 8300[39] with the following additional requirements.

Lift landings should have a change in floor finish contrast and texture from adjacent floor finishes. The change in finish should be completely flush and effectively 'seamless' to prevent a trip hazard and/or possible wear.

The floor of the lift car should contrast with the walls of the car and preferably be a lighter colour so as not to appear like an open lift shaft. All finishes within the car should not produce mirror-like reflections and should be plain.

The movements/action/location of the lift should be given audibly as well as visually. This should include receipt of emergency calls and action taken.

All controls should be tactile as well as being large and contrasting.

The lift car should be evenly illuminated, achieving 100 lux at floor level. The lighting should be fully diffused to avoid glare; spotlights should be avoided.

Adequate sound insulation should be provided to shield adjacent dwellings from noise created by the operation of the lift.

## 16.3.7 Lounge/activity room

The provision of a communal lounge should be discussed with the client.

Where provided, it should be designed as far as possible to have the characteristics of a domestic sitting room, but be adequate for all residents to gather socially.

It should be located off a communal hallway and take advantage of any outlook/give access to any communal garden. It should also be located close to communal toilet facilities.

Any furniture provided should be chosen to provide colour contrast against the floor and wall background colours.

General lighting should maintain an illuminance of 200 lux. Ample sockets should enable additional portable task lighting to be provided at regular locations around the perimeter of the room.

## 16.3.8 Informal seating area(s)

Schemes where residents are likely to be at home during the day should also include an informal seating area located off a communal hallway, possibly in a large bay window or recess that does not interfere with circulation routes, to enable 3–4 residents to meet casually.

## 16.3.9 Laundry

Laundry facilities should be provided if they are not contained in the individual dwellings.

Washing machines and tumble drier numbers should be determined by resident numbers and be of the industrial type.

A dedicated industrial machine/dryer may also be needed for staff use. This potential need should be determined with the client.

A sink and drainer and an adjacent work surface of a minimum 1000 mm should also be provided.

Finishes, colour contrasts, control requirements, etc. are as stated in *Chapter 15* and section 8.3.4.

A clear 1500 mm circulation/activity square should be provided within the room.

The room should not be located adjacent to a private dwelling unless adequate sound insulation and acoustic control is provided to ensure no noise transmission of laundry equipment can be detected within the private dwelling.

Lighting to the laundry should provide a minimum average of 200 lux on the floor surface, and be connected to an individual switch or two-way switching where there are two doors into the laundry room.

Fully diffused task lighting, enabling a 500 lux level on machine controls and work surfaces, should be provided.

## 16.3.10 Stores

Lockable stores should be provided off communal facilities adequate for cleaners' products and tools.

Further full-height general storage should also be provided of at least 1.25 m² floor area.

Schemes where wheelchair and Class 3 vehicle (scooter) use is probable should provide related external or adequately ventilated secure storage with charging facilities.

Additional storage requirements should be discussed and determined with the client according to expected client use for the communal facilities.

Lighting should be provided to stores to enable an illuminance level of 150 lux.

## 16.3.11 Guest accommodation

There may be a need for guest accommodation. This should be discussed with the client. Where provided, its form and scale, should be advised by the client. All provision for guests should follow the relevant requirements of this *Guide*.

## 16.3.12 Lighting

The principles and requirements for lighting stated previously apply to all communal areas.

Automatic switching activated by presence sensors should not be incorporated into hallways (or any other location) as the sudden change in illuminance can be a cause of adaptation problems for some people.

Generally, compact non-flicker fluorescent luminaires, with full diffusers to prevent glare, set against the ceiling finishes are recommended. These should be selected and detailed to provide a domestic, non institutional, appearance.

Lighting in lounges and other communal rooms (not hallways) should be capable of adjustment, for example by providing individual switching to each luminaire or group of luminaires provided. In addition, there should be ample provision of sockets to enable localised task lighting if and when required.

Lamps used within internal fittings should have a colour rendering index of at least Ra80.

Required luminance levels in each communal area are stated elsewhere where the particular requirements for the area/facility are discussed. Zoning and timer controls for potential timed lux level reduction is required as stated.

For ease of maintenance, no fittings are to exceed 2500 mm from finished floor level. In locations where access by step ladders is not safe, the fittings should not exceed a height of 1800 mm from the floor.

### 16.3.13 Heating

The heating specification and performance requirements for communal areas should be discussed and agreed with the client.

The form of heating or positioning of components should avoid any component becoming a bump hazard or obstacle along pedestrian routes. Where the choice of heating includes radiators or other heating components that protrude from finished wall and floor surfaces, it may be necessary to locate them in ducts or recesses.

Where the choice of heating includes radiators, the potential need for low surface temperature types should be discussed and determined with the client.

Requirements are as stated in Chapter 15.

### 16.3.14 Finishes

Ensure all floor finishes are matt and give the required contrast with the walls.

### 16.3.15 Signage

Necessary signage, providing contrasts and tactile information as detailed in the Sign design guide[4] should be provided throughout communal areas.

## Profile 5: Warden back-up gives peace of mind

**Barbara, a middle-aged woman who has had retinitis pigmentosa (RP) since birth, finds that living in an apartment with warden support enables her to retain independence while giving her peace of mind about security.**

Barbara was partially sighted at birth, seeing basic colours, but by 10 years old her sight had deteriorated significantly. She now has only light perception, with extreme sensitivity to artificial and natural light.

Despite having been a working mother to her now grown-up children and enjoying a high degree of self-sufficiency in the past, Barbara now prefers to carry out tasks such as shopping with someone else.

*'The warden's assistance with day-to-day tasks such as correspondence and paperwork is invaluable.'*

Barbara also has a Careline pendant to provide reassurance in case of a fall. An entry system that prevents people she doesn't know from knocking directly on her door adds to Barbara's sense of security. A guide dog also helps her.

*'Maintenance of my previous houses was expensive and difficult as I was not able to carry out or oversee any work myself.'*

Barbara's current property suits her needs far better. The apartment was not designed specifically for people with sight loss, so it had to be adapted. With its warden support, obtaining adaptations has been easier and less expensive than it might otherwise have been.

The adaptations that have been made to Barbara's home include:
* the original strip lighting has been altered and fitted with dimmers as it proved too bright,
* extra standard lamps in her living rooms and dimmer switches,
* a stair gate to indicate the top of the stairs and reduce the risk of a fall,
* lever taps,
* Braille labels for food bags,
* non-slip bathroom flooring,
* tactile stickers,
* talking microwave, scales, kitchen timer and medical thermometer.

There are still some further adaptations that would make Barbara's life easier for the future, eg raising floor-level electrical sockets. Front and rear threshold access could be improved. Currently, for one entrance, adding handrails and a slope to eliminate the step would help. Additional lighting to the rear of the property would add to a sense of security. A support rail at the side of the bath would make having a bath safer.

Barbara prefers to use a supermarket that she is familiar with rather than small shops. She also shops by TV and telephone with the help of friends and relatives. She now prefers to travel by car or taxi as she finds that using public transport is stressful.

She has a support cleaner to clean anything she has missed. A volunteer to help her on a more regular basis would be helpful so that she is less reliant on family and friends.

Overall, Barbara feels that she would not like to move again because her present living arrangements offer such a good level of support.

# APPENDICES

# APPENDIX A
# CONTRAST REQUIREMENTS

For people who have sight loss, the contrast between features and components within their home is of considerable assistance.

Contrast between adjacent surfaces can be achieved either by differences in brightness/luminance or differences in colour/hue or a combination of both.

Although strong differences in colour/hue (eg red, green, blue) can be used to distinguish different features, people with sight loss may have difficulty with discriminating between different colours of similar brightness. The use of different colours of similar brightness can also lead to interiors that appear garish. Differences in lightness, or depth of colour, within a similar hue (eg dark brown against pale cream) also referred to as tonal contrast, can provide a more acceptable solution both in terms of providing a contrast more apparent to people with sight loss, and an overall appearance that is less garish and less 'out of the ordinary'.

The main feature of a surface, which appears to be strongly correlated with the ability of people with sight loss to identify the difference between that surface and an adjacent surface, is the amount of light the surface reflects or its light reflectance value (LRV).

The LRV scale runs from 0 (which is a perfectly absorbing surface that could be assumed to be totally black) up to 100 (which is a perfectly reflective surface that could be considered to be the perfect white). Because of the practical influences of real surfaces black is always greater than 0 and white never equals 100.

The evidence-based research available to date allows a degree of variability concerning the minimum LRV difference that is required to provide adequate visual contrast for people who have sight loss. That variability is shown and described in Appendix G of BS 8300: 2001, 1st Amendment, June 2005[10]. In general, where contrast is very important, a minimum LRV difference of 30 points between the surfaces is recommended. Where contrast is less critical a minimum LRV difference of 20 points is recommended. Differences below 20 points are unlikely to provide adequate contrast.

There is very little research-based evidence concerning the influence of surface textures and multi-coloured surfaces on the contrast required by people with sight loss. However, it is possible to provide subtle interior contrasts that meet the recommendations of BS 8300: 2001[10], provide the necessary minimum LRV difference, and do not appear institutional or garish.

Further guidance is available in: *Colour & contrast – a design guide for the use of colour and contrast to improve the built environment for visually impaired people*[11].

At the time of writing, a new British Standard, BS 8493[12] is being developed.

# APPENDIX B
# TABLE OF RECOMMENDED TASK LIGHTING ILLUMINANCES

The summary recommendations below are drawn from the home studies undertaken as part of the Thomas Pocklington Trust research programme[13]. Table B1 shows the range of illuminances recommended in the area where the task is to be undertaken.

It is important to remember that task lighting should be adjustable in the amount and the distribution of the light to suit the needs of the occupier and these recommendations offer only general guidance. Specific requirements at distinct task areas are given within each functional chapter of this *Guide*. Designers should ensure that the specific requirements stated in the functional chapters are made possible.

| *Table B1:* Recommended task lighting illuminances | | |
| --- | --- | --- |
| **Task definition** | **Examples of activity** | **Recommended illuminance range (lux)** |
| Routine | Showering/bathing | 100–300 |
| | Brushing teeth | 200–300 |
| | Finding keys | 100–300 |
| Time consuming | Writing | 200–1000 |
| | Cooking | 200–1000 |
| | Washing up | 200–500 |
| Short detailed | Choosing clothes (from a drawer) | 100–200 |
| | Using the telephone | 100–400 |
| | Washing (in bathroom) | 100–300 |
| | Putting on shoes | 100–300 |
| Longer detailed | Reading | 200–1000 |
| | Having a meal | 200–500 |
| | Choosing clothes (from a wardrobe) | 100–200 |
| | Choosing clothes (from a drawer) | 100–200 |
| Requiring concentration and presenting a hazard | Making a cup of tea | 200–1000 |
| | Cooking in the kitchen | 200–1000 |

# APPENDIX C
# TABLE OF RECOMMENDED ILLUMINANCES AT THE FLOOR OF EACH ROOM

The summary recommendations given in Table C1 are drawn from the home studies undertaken[13].

The amount of light across the floor of each room as shown in Table C1 is to be considered as an average and determined in accordance with the 'designed maintained illuminance' as defined by the Society of Light and Lighting (SLL) in The Code for Lighting 2004[8]. The recommended SLL values are derived from recommendations for similar areas or areas where similar activities are likely to take place.

Specific illuminance requirements at floor level are given within the functional chapters of this *Guide*. Designers should ensure that the specific requirements stated in the functional chapters are made possible.

**Table C1: Recommended illuminances on the floor of each room**

| Rooms in the home | | Illuminance (lux) Recommended range (Min–Max) | Comparison with recommended SLL value for similar areas | Comparison with BS 8300 recommended minimum value or range |
|---|---|---|---|---|
| Internal area | Hallway | 100–300 | 200 | As SLL |
| | Lounge | 100–300 | 150 | As SLL |
| | Kitchen | 200–300 | 250 | 150–300 |
| | Bathroom | 100–300 | 150 | 100–300 |
| | Bedroom | 100–300 | 100 | 100 |
| | Stairs | 100–200 | 100 | 100 at tread |
| External area | Ramps | 100–200 | 100 | 100 |

# APPENDIX D
# GLOSSARY

**Colour rendering index (Ra)**
A measure of the degree to which the colours of surfaces illuminated by the light from a given light source conform to the colours of the same surfaces under a reference light source.

**Coved skirting**
A concave moulding fixed along the junction between the wall and the floor.

**Crossfall**
A slope on a surface, usually to direct drainage, running in a different direction to the predominant slope on the same surface.

**Dog run**
An enclosed external pen where guide dogs can be taken for toileting, usually provided with drainage and water services.

**Effective clear opening width**
The opening width, measured in the same plane as the wall in which the door is situated, between a line perpendicular to the wall from the outside of the door stop on the door latch side and the nearest obstruction on the hinge side when the door is open. The nearest obstruction may be projecting door furniture, a weatherboard, the door, or the door stop.

**Hazard paving**
A particular form of tactile underfoot paving, in the pattern of half-rod-shaped bars (sometimes called corduroy), to give warning of a potential hazard that requires caution. *Note:* This is just one form of tactile underfoot paving. Each different form provides different detectable contrasts in surface textures and pattern. Each texture and pattern has a distinct meaning, should be exclusively reserved for its intended use and consistently installed in accordance with recognised guidelines.

**Handed dwelling**
A dwelling with a floor layout that is identical to another dwelling but is a mirror-image of that other dwelling's floor layout.

**Hue**
The apparently dominant part of the spectrum occupied by a colour (eg red as distinct from yellow or blue).

| | |
|---|---|
| Intrusive light | The intrusion of over-bright or poorly directed lights onto a neighbouring property which affect the neighbour's right to enjoy their own property. A typical example would be an inconsiderately directed security light shining onto a neighbour's window. |
| IP rating | The Ingress Protection (IP) number of a luminaire is a two-digit number describing the level of protection offered by the luminaire against the ingress of dust and moisture. |
| Light reflectance value (LRV) | The proportion of the light falling on a surface that is reflected by that surface. |
| Luminance | Physical measure of the stimulus which produces the sensation of brightness. |
| Illuminance | Luminous flux density on a surface, ie the amount of light falling on a surface per unit surface area. |
| Light pollution | Artifical light that is allowed to illuminate, or pollute, areas not intended to be lit. |
| Stair/step nosing | The edge of the stair/step where the riser meets the tread. |
| Stair/step riser | The upright face of a stair/step. |
| Stair/step going | The horizontal distance between two successive nosings on a flight of stairs/steps. |
| Stair winders | A tread of triangular or wedge shape, changing the direction of a stair. |
| Street furniture | A collective term for items such as benches, litter bins, lamp posts, bollards, signs, planters, etc. placed on footpaths and landscaping in a communal or semi-communal environment. |

# REFERENCES AND FURTHER READING

REFERENCES

[1] **Thomas Pocklington Trust.** *Prevalence, causes and impact of sight loss in older people in Britain*. Occasional paper 8. London, Thomas Pocklington Trust, June 2006

[2] **Weale RA.** *The aging eye.* London, HK Lewis, 1963

[3] **Thorpe S & Habinteg Housing Association.** *Wheelchair housing design guide* (2nd edition). Bracknell, IHS BRE Press, 2006

[4] **Barker P & Fraser J.** *Sign design guide.* London, JMU Access Partnership and the Sign Design Society, 2000

[5] **Association of Chief Police Officers (ACPO).** *Secured by design.* London, ACPO Crime Prevention Initiatives. 2004. www.securedbydesign.com

[6] **The Institution of Lighting Engineers.** *Guidance notes for the reduction of obtrusive light.* Rugby, ILE, 2005

[7] **Department for Transport.** *Guidance on the use of tactile paving surfaces.* Updated June 2007. Available from www.dft.gov.uk/transportforyou/access/tipws

[8] **Society of Light and Lighting (SLL).** *SLL Code for Lighting.* London, CIBSE, 2006. Available as CD ROM from www.cibse.org

[9] **(Department for) Communities and Local Government (CLG).** *The Building Regulations 2000. Approved Document M: Access to and use of buildings.* 2004 edition. Available from www.planningportal.gov.uk

[10] **British Standards Institution.** BS 8300: 2001: *Design of buildings and their approaches to meet the needs of disabled people. Code of practice.* London, BSI

[11] **ICI Dulux.** *Colour & contrast — a design guide for the use of colour and contrast to improve the built environment for visually impaired people.* Slough, ICI Dulux

**[12] British Standards Institution.** BS 8493: *Method of test for determining contrast.* London, BSI, 2008 (to be published)

**[13] Percival J.** *Lighting the homes of people with sight loss: an overview of recent research. Occasional paper 13.* London, Thomas Pocklington Trust, July 2007

**FURTHER READING**

**Barker P, Barrick J & Wilson R.** *Building sight.* London, RNIB and HMSO, 1995

**Carroll C, Cowans J & Darton D.** *Meeting Part M and designing Lifetime Homes.* York, Joseph Rowntree Foundation

**Foundations, National Coordinating Body for Home Improvement Agencies & Centre for Housing Policy, University of York.** *Delivering home improvement agency services to visually impaired people: A good practice guide.* London, Thomas Pocklington Trust & Collective Enterprises, 2003

**Foundations, National Coordinating Body for Home Improvement Agencies & Centre for Housing Policy, University of York.** *Effective HIA services for visually impaired people: a development project 2002–3.* London, Thomas Pocklington Trust, June 2003

**Habinteg Housing Association.** *Design guide.* London, Habinteg Housing Association, 2003

**Habinteg Housing Association.** *Realities of independent living — supported housing design guidance.* London, Habinteg Housing Association, 2005

**Habinteg Housing Association, GML Architects & Mayor of London.** *Lifetime Homes — Living well together.* London, Habinteg Housing Association

**Hanson J.** *Meeting the housing and support needs of people aged 18–55 with sight loss: A good practice guide for housing providers in the sight loss sector.* Good Practice Guide 1. London, Thomas Pocklington Trust, 2006

**Hanson J.** *The housing and support needs of people aged 18–55 with sight loss.* Occasional paper 7. London, Thomas Pocklington Trust, February 2006

**Hanson J et al.** *Housing and support needs of older people with sight loss – experiences and challenges.* Occasional paper 1 (2nd edition). London, Thomas Pocklington Trust, February 2006

**Hanson J, Johnson M, Percival J & Zako R.** *The housing, care and support needs of older people with visual impairments living in a variety of settings.* Volumes 1 & 2. London, Thomas Pocklington Trust, 2002

**O'Neill L.** *Lighting the homes of people with sight loss.* Occasional paper 4. London, Thomas Pocklington Trust, October 2003

**Percival J.** *Meeting the needs of older people with visual impairment; social care or social exclusion?* Occasional paper 2. London, Thomas Pocklington Trust, October 2003

**PRP Architects.** *Design guide for the development of new build accommodation for older people.* St Albans, The Abbeyfield Society, 2001

**Rees L & Lewis C.** *Housing sight.* Cardiff, RNIB Cymru and the Welsh Assembly Government, October 2003

**Rees L & Lewis C.** *Adapting homes.* Cardiff, RNIB Cymru and Welsh Assembly Government, 2003

**Ricability and Housing Corporation.** *Taking control.* London, Ricability and Housing Corporation, 2004

**Robson D, Nicholson A-M & Barker N.** *Homes for the third age — a design guide for extra care sheltered housing.* London, E & FN Spon, 1997

**Thomas Pocklington Trust.** *Lighting the homes of people with sight loss.* Research findings 3. London, Thomas Pocklington Trust, October 2003

**Thomas Pocklington Trust.** *The housing and support needs of people aged 18–55 with sight loss.* Research findings 11. London, Thomas Pocklington Trust, December 2005

**Thomas Pocklington Trust.** *Lighting at home for independence and safety.* London, Thomas Pocklington Trust, April 2006

# INDEX